SCHOOL DECISION-MAKING

School Decision-Making

Educational Management in Secondary Schools

CYRIL POSTER
Headmaster, The Sheppey School, Kent

HEINEMANN EDUCATIONAL BOOKS
LONDON

Heinemann Educational Books Ltd

LONDON EDINBURGH MELBOURNE AUCKLAND TORONTO
HONG KONG SINGAPORE KUALA LUMPUR IBADAN NAIROBI
JOHANNESBURG LUSAKA NEW DELHI
KINGSTON

ISBN 0 435 80640 8

First published 1976

Published by
Heinemann Educational Books Ltd
48 Charles Street, London W1X 8AH
Printed in Great Britain by
Cox & Wyman Ltd, London, Fakenham and Reading

Contents

To my staff, past and present,
my sternest critics and staunchest supporters,
and to my family,
not least those who mowed the lawn so that
I could get on with my writing

Foreword

As more and more care has been given to the organization of schools, and all that is implied by that seemingly simple word, the need for the *Heinemann Organization in Schools Series* has been more and more strongly expressed. The quality of the secondary-school experience is of great importance to our society and to those who are pupils. Never before has the professional challenge to those who are teachers been so great. The series is a systematic attempt to help schools improve the quality of that experience by a methodical study of the ways schools can be organized.

The series has been planned as a whole, so that the central philosophy and every aspect of the planning and running of a secondary, especially comprehensive, school is methodically covered. However, each book has been written by a different author out of his or her own observation, experience, and conviction to stand on its own as a complete volume. Inevitably, and deliberately, this means that there is some overlapping between the volumes as certain topics (such as pupil choice, or a school's relationship with parents) are explored in a number of books, though with varying degrees of detail and from different points of view.

We have a number of different readers in mind – especially senior staff and headteachers actually concerned with the practical day-to-day decisions, but also those many teachers ambitious to hold such positions, and, indeed, students and others interested in the endlessly fascinating question of how schools are run. The series aims to strengthen practice with theory and to enliven theory with practice, above all to be *useful*.

Every volume in the series has attempted to chart some of the possible decisions that a school has to make in various aspects of its work. This book, as its title suggests, is about actually how those decisions can be made. It is thus central to the series, for the decision-making process of a school itself needs the most careful planning if the school is to be a successful learning community.

As the book makes clear, there is no single 'right' way, but from the experience of the growth of comprehensive schools a great deal can be learnt to help on-going schools adjust and improve their management patterns and to help newly reorganized schools set up theirs.

Cyril Poster is able to draw on his own considerable experience as a well-known headmaster of two contrasting schools. Thus his arguments and illustrations are essentially those of a man involved in helping to make a school work. However, he supports this by the results of extensive reading and close observation. A special feature of the book is the way in which Mr Poster has been able to use the case studies of a number of management courses that he has run over the years. More than that, the reactions of course members, their questions, and their discussions have enriched the argument and the details of the book.

The organization of a modern comprehensive school depends on suitable management structures and effective decision-making procedures. Decisions are the core of school management, and *School Decision-Making* is a realistic and humane discussion of how they might be made.

MICHAEL MARLAND

Preface

It is customary for authors of non-fiction to apologize for inflicting on the public 'yet another book' on a particular topic. I make no such apology for this book. Almost all the literature on secondary-school management comes from *outside* the sphere with which it deals; and while I freely acknowledge my indebtedness to writers and researchers in higher education, I believe that there is a great need for a book written entirely from the point of view of someone 'in the field'.

I had been contemplating a book on secondary-school management for a year or so before I left Lawrence Weston School, Bristol, at the end of 1969. It was then that I first devised, in collaboration with Dick Ashman (at that time my senior master, and later headmaster of Edgecliff School, Kinver, Staffordshire), the Kinslade School simulation. Since that time we have together and separately conducted in various parts of the country at least a dozen workshop courses built around this newly reorganized 12 to 16 comprehensive school. Though fictitious, it is far from fictional, since all the management problems we present are drawn from experience.

I owe Dick Ashman a debt that he would be the first to decry, but which nevertheless is considerable. He has been my friend, colleague, workhorse and, when necessary, critic for many years. To those who have been our course tutors, especially Pat Creek, headmistress of Hadleigh School, Suffolk, and Hugh Colgate, headmaster of Buckhurst Hill County High School, Essex, I must pay tribute for the wisdom, experience and unstinting effort they have contributed. Because these have been workshop courses we have learnt as much from the students as they have from us. Of no one is this more true than of Mervyn Saunders, now head-master of Siddal Moor High School, Heywood, from whom I learnt much about the potential use of critical path analysis in educational management.

The material for this book was beginning to assemble itself in innumerable folders on and around my desk at home when Michael Marland invited me to contribute to this series. Though I was now deeply committed to the establishment of a new large comprehensive school in Kent – indeed probably because I was so involved in just those managerial problems with which such a book must deal – I accepted with alacrity. Inevitably, because my understanding of the problems has grown during the time of writing, the book has grown too.

Many people have contributed to the writing of this book, far more than I can mention here. Ron Glatter of London University Institute of Education gave me valuable encouragement in the early stages, and I acknowledge my debt to his book *Management Development for the Education Profession*. Bob Glover, Principal of Portslade School and Community College, East Sussex; Geoffrey Holroyde, formerly Principal of Sidney Stringer School and Community College, Coventry, and now Director of Lanchester Polytechnic; John Watts, Principal of Countesthorpe Community College, Leicestershire; Derek Saville and David Styan, headmasters of Marple Hall and Marple Ridge High Schools, Stockport, respectively – all these have been most generous in allowing me to refer freely to the role definitions and structures of their establishments. Valerie Perry, headmistress of Wilbraham School, Manchester, kindly gave me leave to quote material from an article in *Secondary Education*, published by the National Union of Teachers. Martin Haney of Portland Community College, Oregon, while in Kent as an exchange teacher obtained for me valuable material on teacher assessment.

Some have been unwitting contributors, in that I have needed examples of bad management practice as well as good. I trust that I have suitably disguised their contributions and have offended nobody.

Ellen Stupple, June West and Wendy Bridges transformed hundreds of pages of barely legible manuscript into highly accurate typescript. Bruce Brand, at the time of writing a sixth-year student at the Sheppey School, contributed the amusing cartoons in the *Kemshire Newsheet*. Janet Friedlander, of the National Union of Teachers Library, has helped greatly, obtaining books from strange places in days and finding references over the telephone in minutes.

My wife's contribution to this book is beyond measure. She has read its pages repeatedly, listened to so many lectures I have given and discussions I have led, tolerated my untidiness, and has always been on hand with advice and support.

1 Management and education

Educational management is not a skill reserved for the professional élite. It is the concern of every teacher. The newly qualified teacher, confronted by his first class, has before him the task of managing his resources, his environment and his pupils. Properly, his management of all three should have preceded his confrontation. Anticipation of the situation is vital to sound managerial control. However, in schools, whatever the degree of our experience, we repeatedly encounter unknown factors we are unlikely to have anticipated, and adaptation to the situation is no less important.

'I went into my first teaching practice lesson,' confided a candidate for a post recently, 'with an hour's work prepared. I used it all up in five minutes. For fifty-five minutes I had to flannel like mad. Never again, I promised myself.'

'It was a wonderful lesson,' said a probationer teacher, 'on paper, at any rate. A ten-minute session of mime was to have provided the stimulus for a session of creative writing on the same theme. I asked them to clear some space in the middle of the classroom for the mime. I am sure they meant well, because they were obviously enthusiastic for the work, but they took ten minutes to do it, and even then the room looked as if it had been struck by a hurricane. During that ten minutes I had to go to the teacher in the next classroom to apologize for the noise; the deputy head came in to see whether he could help me to control the class; and the caretaker passed by with a look of resignation on his face – but what kind of "resignation" I was not too sure. We never did get on to the creative writing . . .'

A list of the classroom teacher's involvement with the school-management structure, even for the relatively 'simple' task of doing his job, is sufficiently formidable:

the timetable, procedure for room changes, cover for absent staff;

the syllabus, the degree of control it imposes or the latitude it provides, its relationship, structured or fortuitous, with those in other subjects;

resources, where they are kept, how they are issued, what facilities are available for their preparation, what constraints have to be imposed;

procedures for pupils absent from lessons, for control problems, for sudden sickness, for fire alarms . . .

The list continues. In many schools it extends to a volume of reference, entitled *Handbook for Staff* and presented to the new arrival before his first term in the school begins.

Even in the degree to which he successfully operates the school's managerial practice, the classroom teacher is contributing to control of the situation. In his relationships with his pupils he is involved in aspects of the psychology and sociology of management – *motivation* and *group behaviour* in particular. As much might be said about his involvement with his colleagues. Every school is an institution and every institution has a structure, explicit or implicit. The teacher's place in that structure will influence his interpersonal relationships, and his contentment, or otherwise, with that place will be one of the factors influencing his performance and his job satisfaction.

The more senior teacher's managerial responsibilities go beyond those of the classroom teacher. He is responsible not merely for himself and his pupils, but for other staff and theirs. He learns to appreciate that the successful running of a school depends on its aims and objectives and that these are capable of being given precision. He learns too, often the hard way, that any ideas that he might hold to be of value cannot be put into effect by edict. He may command, but are the troops following? He begins to understand the place in management of consultation and communication.

With the headteacher rests the ultimate responsibility, for it is he who will determine the priorities of management. Because it is impossible to advance on all fronts at once, it is he who must decide which are most vulnerable, or most productive. He must 'orchestrate' progress so that the school develops as an entity, even if in doing so he finds it necessary to hold back in certain areas in order to achieve consolidation in others. He must take the long-term view, in order to achieve consistency and stability in the organization, without which the organization becomes a mere sum of its parts, and the loss of a part leads to the dissolution of

the organization. Stability, however, must never become stag-
nation. A school is a dynamic structure in a changing world, and
to stand still is to go backwards.

The headteacher commands the distribution of the resources of
management: the allocation of staff, posts of responsibility,
finance, and so on. Though he is controlled by the local education
authority in the amount at his disposal, he retains the power to
change the course of a school's development by the policy he
adopts.

Above all, he determines the style of management: charismatic,
traditional or bureaucratic, to use the terminology of Max Weber;[1]
or somewhere along the spectrum between two 'ideal types' of
management called by Tom Burns[2] *mechanistic* and *organic*. (I
will return shortly to a more detailed study of the latter.)

The application of business management to education

In spite of Musgrove's statement that schools and industrial
organizations 'belong to the same "family" and have common
characteristics',[3] there are grave dangers in the wholesale application of business management theory and techniques to education.
There is some evidence of this danger in the upsurge of interest
in schools of business management in some polytechnics and
universities for mounting courses for educationists. The very
language used is sufficient indication that educational management is being approached 'from the outside'. The syllabus for one
such course on the management of large secondary schools has a
section called 'The efficient use of manpower resources' which is
subdivided:

    (i)   Manpower planning and analysis of needs;
    (ii) Job analysis, job description, and man specifications;
    (iii) Recruitment and selection;
    (iv) Methods of developing staff, training and induction;
    (v) Methods of staff appraisal.

There is, in fact, not one item there (except for 'man specifications'
which stirs up echoes of Frankenstein's clandestine activities)

---

[1] Max Weber, *The Theory of Social and Economic Organisation* (Free
Press, 1947).

[2] T. Burns and G. M. Stalker, *The Management of Innovation* (Tavistock,
1968).

[3] F. Musgrove, *Patterns of Power and Authority in English Education*
(Methuen, 1971).

which does not find a place in this book. Yet the whole approach is utterly alien to the kinds of relationships that are necessary in a school if it is to function effectively.

Management theory can be of value to education if it is first assimilated and only then applied. It is interesting to compare with the section of the course syllabus just quoted the words of a headmaster who had probably a greater direct knowledge of industrial management theory and practice than anyone in charge of a school. In a paper on management and organization prepared for the staff of the Sidney Stringer School and Community College, Geoffrey Holroyde makes the statement:

> A situation full of change and of the unknown calls for a flexible and dynamic approach, and although it is necessary to design an organisation structure to indicate in some measure the relationships between people, strict adherence to a mechanistic and authoritarian system would slow down the decision-making and inhibit initiative. It is imagined that the structure will be organic, and that groups of people will cooperate with each other to identify and solve problems ...

Holroyde's use of the terms 'mechanistic' and 'organic' takes us back to the management theory of Tom Burns. Burns defines the mechanistic type of organization as suitable to stable conditions, to a hierarchical management structure in which there is a clear definition of assigned roles, formal and mainly vertical communication, and a built-in system of checks and supervision. In such a system, because the overall strategy is known only at the top, innovation from the grass-roots is unlikely. Advancement within such an organization tends to depend not on merit, but on long service and conformity.

The organic type of organization, on the other hand, is designed to adapt to a rapid rate of change, to situations in which 'new and unfamiliar problems continually arise which cannot be broken down and distributed among the existing specialist roles.'[1] Relationships are therefore lateral rather than vertical, and form and reform according to the demands of the particular problem. Innovation may occur at any level, and will be a product of the greater commitment to and understanding of the overall aims of the organization.

Holroyde's enthusiasm for an organic structure, appropriate as it may be to the school he was establishing, should not blind one to difficulties inherent in its widespread application. First, *existing*

[1] Pugh, Hickson and Hinings, eds, *Writers on Organisations* (Penguin, 1971).

structures which are largely mechanistic cannot become organic by decree. Indeed, the very nature of authoritarian control implicit in the formal structure makes change tantamount to knocking away the lame man's crutches from under him. Better to walk with crutches than to fall flat on your face. Secondly, the organic structure requires a particular style of leadership. There are utopian assumptions behind 'groups of people' co-operating with each other 'to identify and solve problems'.

Since we are dealing with a structure with a high rate of change we would be wise not to take for granted the adaptability of the members of the organization. It is perfectly legitimate for those who subscribe to the same set of aims nevertheless to differ over the route to be taken in achieving those aims. For any organization is the sum of its component parts: people. Just as an apparently stable mechanistic organization may break down under stress, in particular the failure of top management to demonstrate that it is wholly in charge of the situation, so an organic structure may fail when there is irreconcilable conflict over objectives. Burns argues that any organization is 'the simultaneous working of at least three social systems. The first of these is the formal authority system derived from the aims of the organisation . . . But organisations are also cooperative systems of people who have career aspirations and a career structure, and who compete for advancement.' Finally, 'every organisation is the scene of "political" activity in which individuals and departments compete and cooperate for power.'[1]

It is not difficult to perceive that schools are no less subject to the working of these three social systems than industrial undertakings. The main difference is that the organizational aims are likely to be couched in idealistic terms, because a school's 'success' is not measurable in cost-effectiveness or productivity; that career aspirations have their outlet far more within the educational system than within the school itself, and that therefore competition for advancement is not so powerful as in industry; and that the security of tenure enjoyed within the teaching profession, while it may act as a brake on progress, is also a disincentive to the power struggle.

Aims and Objectives

'Aims'n'objectives' has become a portmanteau phrase, given an airing every time someone seeks to encapsulate the philosophy

[1] op. cit., pages 46–7.

that determines the direction in which a particular institution seeks to go. Unless we use the words with greater precision in educational management, we are in danger of debasing language and obscuring thought.

Aims can be either long-term or short-term. Long-term aims tend to be an expression of utopian ideals: *to develop to the full each child's intellectual, social, moral and spiritual potential.* Such an aim is not to be derided. The danger is that, because such an aim is so obviously unattainable, and because teachers are no more able to pursue this aim in isolation than are, say, parents or ministers of religion, it becomes merely a pious aspiration. It may be that the best we can hope to be is 'encouragers' and that aims such as this are valid more in that they indicate a direction, than because they posit an absolute:

> One is bound to think of one's aims as a teacher in terms of the 'end-product': what sort of men and women would we like to send out into the world? A person who has become aware of his or her potential, has gone some way towards fulfilling it, and will try to continue doing so, in study and in leisure; who has not been labelled a failure because of shortcomings in one respect; who cares deeply about fellow human beings and aims to do something in their service; who has been taught to think about society, to ask questions about it and, where it is found wanting, to try to improve it; one who is capable of warm human relationships, who is resilient in the face of set-backs and frustrations; one who will be able to cope with the ever-growing pace of change in a technological society.[1]

Short-term aims are by their nature more readily defined and open to evaluation: *to establish the machinery for the fullest possible staff participation in decision-making.* Such an aim does not presuppose that the ideal system can be established immediately, or even that the system which best suits one stage in the development of an institution will remain best suited to a later stage of development. Nevertheless it soon becomes apparent whether this aim is a 'statement of intent' or a façade behind which the system will operate as before.

There is a tendency to equate aims with horizons. The danger of this equation is that horizons recede as we approach them, and advance as we move away from them. Educational horizons have few if any completely objective landmarks. It is easy therefore and decidedly fashionable for certain educationists and politicians

[1] From a paper 'Some Ideas on Aims' prepared by Dr F. D. Rushworth, headmaster of Holland Park School, for discussion by the staff.

to call for a return to 'standards' of attainment or behaviour in schools, implying that these standards are identifiable and measurable. It is no less easy, on the other hand, for inadequacies to be hidden beneath a cloak of mystique and verbiage.

Similarly aims should be distinguished from principles. Principles are immutable. As a Quaker I believe that there is 'that of God in every man'. This is a belief I share with many educationists, though they may, either as members of other religious bodies or as humanists, express themselves in different terms. This principle rules my life in so far as I am able to live up to it. It will certainly colour the aims that I personally would establish for a school; but it would not prevent me from modifying those aims in the light of experience, provided I was not called upon to depart from my principles.

Finally, aims and objectives are often likened to strategy and tactics. Perhaps the reader need only be reminded of the dictum that tactics win battles, strategy loses wars!

Objectives are the stepping-stones by which aims will be realized or approached. There are likely to be two sets of objectives: institutional objectives and sectional objectives. It is the task of management to harness and harmonize the two.

First, the objectives of the institution need to be analysed to determine the contribution to be made by the sections. For example, a school may decide that it wishes to move away from formal examinations at the end of the fifth year of secondary education and towards continuous assessment covering the whole of the fourth and fifth years. To set this up as a school objective without examining its effect on each area of the syllabus would be irresponsible. Each subject area needs to examine this objective in the light of its own resources, the adaptability of its staff to new responsibilities, the advantages and disadvantages to the students of change. For some subjects the new objectives will be readily acceptable, requiring only a modification of present practice. For others it may involve major and disruptive change and be untimely or undesirable. The institutional objectives will not be vitiated by a gradualist approach, and the experience of one section in attaining its objectives may benefit another.

Secondly, a section's objectives need to be analysed to determine their effect on other sections and on the institution as a whole. This is particularly true in a school which conforms to the organic organizational pattern. Decentralized innovation may, imperceptibly, lead to a conflict of objectives even when they appear to subscribe to the same aim. It may be that there is a difference in interpretation, one man's freedom of thought being another man's permissiveness. It may be that the objectives of one section make an undue demand on scarce resources of manpower, time or materials. It may simply be that the consequences of a sectional initiative have not been appreciated, either by the section or by the school as a whole. It is axiomatic that, without the harmonious interrelationship of sectional objectives, there can be no sound institutional objectives.

Management by objectives

The devolution of responsibility implicit in less hierarchical institutional structures requires, therefore, some checks and balances. Management has the task of organizing human and material resources to achieve satisfactory performance. This it can best do, Drucker[1] claims, by translating aims into a series of specific tasks. Because these tasks have limited objectives, they can be evaluated. Indeed, the soundness of a management decision can even be assessed while it is being made, because there is a framework of reference against which to make judgements.

It can be argued that 'management by objectives' is a theory applicable to industrial efficiency, but not to education since we are dealing largely with intangibles. It may be that educationists sometimes tend to hide deficiencies in the system behind a smoke-screen of abstractions; but the dangers of channelling assessment of performance solely or largely to that which can easily be measured are of far greater concern. Stuart Maclure[2] writes of the 'attempts now being made in every U.S. state to introduce "accountability" programmes for . . . schools'. He reports on the investigation of the Centre for Educational Research and Curriculum Evaluation of the University of Illinois into such assessment schemes:

> What seems clear – and highly relevant to any formal move to introduce such practices in England – is that the all-important question is not whether effective measures of efficiency can be designed, but what use you make of such measures once they are available.
>
> The more sophisticated schemes start with a search for what are called criterion-referenced tests. These purport to measure achievement against the stated objectives of the system, not against norms

[1] Peter Drucker's ideas are admirably summarized in the section 'The management of organisations' in *Writers on Organisations*.

[2] In 'American Diary', the *Times Educational Supplement* (28 March 1975).

of current practice. So a lot of work goes into establishing objectives and *translating them into specific levels of competence which
can be measured.* Of course, in practice, the objectives which are
first considered are those concerned *with a narrow range of learning in the basic skills.* [My italics]

This abuse of the technique of management by objectives does
not invalidate the technique itself. Management by objectives
remains a useful tool whereby aspiration can be evaluated against
performance.

Indeed the value to education of management by objectives
probably lies far more in its psychological effect than its prag-
matic results. It is, after all, a challenge to those in what, in a
hierarchical system, would be called 'subordinate' roles to identify
their goals for themselves and their co-workers, and to evaluate
their performance. There is strong evidence that involvement in
decision-making and managerial self-control reduces tension,
interdepartmental rivalry and friction. When you design the can
yourself, it is far more difficult to get out of carrying it.[1] Because
communication is essential to the devolution of responsibility
implicit in such a management system, there is a diminution of
the we–they syndrome: where there are no 'in-groups' there can
be no 'out-groups'.

Strong support for management by objectives *in the context of
an organic organizational structure* is to be found in the work of a
number of writers on social psychology. Their thinking is best
summarized by the editors of *Management and Motivation.*[2]
Participative management 'assumes that individuals can derive
satisfaction from doing an effective job *per se*'. One element in
participative management is 'the reduction in the use of authority
as a means of control'.

> [The manager] is there as a resource for his subordinate to use,
> but he resists imposing his ideas on his subordinates concerning
> how their jobs should be done . . . On matters affecting the entire
> unit [he] does not make decisions autocratically and issue orders

[1] 'When we fail to achieve the result we desire, we tend to seek the
cause everywhere but where it usually lies: in our choice of inappropriate
methods of control . . . When people respond to managerial decisions in
undesired ways, the normal response is to blame them. It is *their* stupidity,
or *their* uncooperativeness, or *their* laziness which is seized on as the
explanation of what happened . . .' D. M. McGregor, *The Human Side of
Enterprise* (McGraw-Hill, 1960).

[2] *Management and Motivation,* ed. V. H. Vroom and E. L. Deci (Penguin,
1970).

to his subordinates, but rather he meets with his subordinates as a group and shares problems with them and encourages them to participate with him in finding solutions to these problems.

The relevance of this to educational management is fourfold. As will be seen in the chapters that follow, the growing complexity of the task of management makes it no longer possible for any headteacher himself *efficiently* to control all the facets of the organization in his charge. Even if he is unwilling to relinquish the reins of absolute authority, there is a rising groundswell of dissatisfaction within the teaching profession against this concentration of power. There must be a recognizable conformity between the management style of a school and the environment of learning: open-ended learning situations, for example, cannot thrive in an authoritarian regime. Finally, if there is to be communal concern for education, involvement in the process of management must be widespread and understanding of it manifest.

2 Organization and roles

The power of the headteacher of a school is unquestionable. Provided he keeps within the conditions of his articles of government and does not so offend against the law of the land that the Department of Education and Science is led to question his competence, once appointed he is there, if he so wishes, until retirement. He may be absolute dictator of curricular policy, deciding what subjects will be taught, in what manner, for how many periods a week, and beginning at what age. He may decree that his schools will be streamed, banded or unstreamed. He may decide which pupils will enter for what examination. He may be the arbiter of fashion, determining the length of hair or skirt that his pupils may wear, and he has been known to prohibit the wearing of national dress by immigrant minorities, though that dress may have religious or moral significance to the wearer. He may legislate within his school on codes of conduct, and according to his views produce in his mixed school the absurdity of all girls being addressed by their forenames and all boys by their surnames. A headmaster may decide that *his* is a rugby school or a soccer school. A headmistress may decide that athletics is an unladylike pursuit and exclude it from the physical education programme. A school may gain a reputation for fencing, handwriting, chess, or drama because of the head's own interest in a particular activity and the resources he is prepared to divert to it. Above all, though he has no absolute powers over the engagement of teaching staff, he can so advertise, allocate posts of responsibility and, to be brutally frank, manipulate, that he can surround himself by staff who will see things his way.

That the headteacher has by law and established practice very wide powers indeed is beyond doubt. An increasing number of people, both within the profession and without, are challenging this. It matters not at all, they claim, that this power may be used benevolently: it is not its intention which is in question, but its justification in the social context of the present day. A school cannot be educating for the future with the materials and structures of the past.

Others see those who want to reduce the power of the head-teacher as dangers to the Establishment, and castigate them, in their terms, as being 'left-wing', 'social engineers', 'egalitarians'. Angus Maude conjures up the spectre of the educationist who:

> complains bitterly of the excessive 'competitiveness' of the con-ventional system of education, and claims that his reforms would remove the 'stresses' from which children are alleged to suffer. Not only does he dislike class marks and competitive examinations, he has a horror of any test which some children might fail. This leads him on to decry the importance of academic standards and discipline – and indeed of learning itself.[1]

This argument, that 'modern' education is undermining the social fabric, is age-old. For corrupting the young, Socrates was put to death. It would be flattering to the ego to think that education might be so effective that our schools and universities would bring about radical social change by the teaching methods and organi-zational structures they adopted. There are those, moreover, who argue that it is the duty of our educational system to promote an order which our society is currently lacking, to strengthen 'the national will to transmit to future generations those values, standards and aspirations which made England admired the world over'.[2] If one accepts this view of educational objectives, it may be reasonable to expect our schools to seek to maintain the decision-making structures of a past society. Yet, even assuming that it was desirable, is it any longer possible? When Dewey wrote 'The development within the young of the attitudes and disposi-tions necessary to the continuous and progressive life of a society . . . takes place through the intermediary of the environment', he did not merely force the school out of its restrictive physical and intellectual confines into contact with the realities and ideas of society. He allowed the incursion of elements from society which were to produce an irreversible chemical change in the nature of education.

What takes place in our schools and what happens in society are therefore directly related. Whether we stand like Canute on

---

[1] 'The Egalitarian Threat', Angus Maude's contribution to *Fight for Education*, better known as Black Paper No. 1, ed. C. B. Cox and A. E. Dyson (Critical Quarterly Society, 1969).

[2] From the speech 'Britain: a decadent New Utopia' made by Sir Keith Joseph in October 1974, as reprinted in the *Guardian* (21 October 1974).

the beach or rush headlong into the surf, the tide will still flow. Canute undoubtedly suffered as the waves lapped over his sandals, but the danger of being swept out of our depth by the undertow is decidedly greater. Swimming demands certain managerial skills: principally an understanding of the nature of the environment – the water – and an appreciation of the pull of the currents one will encounter; and the coherent organization of the resources available, at worst to keep the body afloat, at best to make progress.

Leadership and responsibility

In our present society there are very few structures which can maintain a stable existence based solely on collective responsibility, without any form of leadership. Within the counter-culture, the commune appears at times to be such a structure. In *Youthquake*,[1] a book which depicts the counter-culture with remarkable sympathy and insight, the author illustrates the appalling and rapid degeneration within a few years of the Haight-Ashbury community, which began as the mecca of the flower-children and became the hideout of the addict and the drug trafficker. Small communes may maintain greater stability, particularly those which withdraw from society. They achieve this in most cases by substituting an idealism, mystical or social, often both, for overt leadership.

It would be wrong to identify the Israeli kibbutzim with the counter-culture, since they are very much a product of the social policy of the people of that country. Nevertheless they bear comparison with the communes in their form of organization through collective responsibility, and their attitude to leadership. Bruno Bettelheim,[2] while drawing distinctions between those kibbutzim motivated by political and those by religious ideology, nevertheless indicates that 'all kibbutzim share a like way of organising the life of the child . . . in which the collective idea has triumphed over the concrete person and where the family no longer serves as mediator between society and the child.' With young people in particular, peer-group pressure becomes as much a straitjacket as any set of adult authoritarian regulations. It may be that this peer-group pressure is more realistic and acceptable than that of adult society; but Bettelheim suggests that it is, in its own way, as rigidly demanding of conformity as an imposed authoritarian

[1] Kenneth Leech, *Youthquake* (Sheldon Press, 1973).
[2] Bruno Bettelheim, *The Children of the Dream* (Thames and Hudson, 1969).

regime. The leadership may be collective, but it is no more accepting of the deviant than the most highly structured hierarchical society. What the collective leadership believes to be right is 'what the Kibbutz wants'; and the desire of the Kibbutz is invested with a significance which, understandable in view of the history of the Jews since the Diaspora, is quasi-mystical.

For educationalists there is little precedent for any system which is not dependent on those structures which society generates. Here, interestingly, there is little difference in practice between the structures of capitalist and communist society. If anything, communist education seems to be more rigidly directed than capitalist education, in spite of the enthusiastic expectations of early post-war writers such as Beatrice King.[1] Indeed, with the exception of some very interesting state-sponsored experiments in Yerres, near Paris, and 't Karregat in Eindhoven, Holland,[2] and the alternative schools in Seattle, we have to look outside the normal state systems for even the merest shreds of evidence of the success or failure of genuine collective responsibility in educational establishments.

In this country the achievement of collective responsibility without overt leadership has been confined to a very few highly experimental schools, all of them in the private sector, such as A. S. Neil's Summerhill, or, on the fringe of the state system, those brave attempts to involve the maladjusted or anti-social child on the lines of Homer Lane's Little Commonwealth. Nor is this surprising. The history of English education is of the expansion to the masses, in a series of education acts which always succeed a war or major social upheaval, of the form of education previously reserved for the privileged. In a society as marked for its social divisiveness and hierarchical structure as the Hindu caste system, though decidedly more subtly, it was inevitable that schools should be rigidly stratified.

Styles of leadership

Ronald King describes in 'The head teacher and his authority'[3] the headmaster who relies on what he calls 'ritualistic authority'.

> [He is] likely to have a system of prefects, to act as general models of school-accepted behaviour and agents of social control. He may

---

[1] Beatrice King, *Russia Goes to School* (Heinemann, 1948).

[2] See the articles by Ekelijn ter Haar and Bertus Mulder in *Jeugden Samenleving* (January 1974).

[3] Chapter 6 of *Headship in the 1970s*, ed. Bryan Allen (Blackwell, 1968).

induct them in a ceremony in which the passing of some of his authority to them is symbolised by his shaking hands with them, and the award of a distinctive tie or badge. The ritualised head-teacher can delegate authority in this way. Even teachers may use the threat of such a headteacher to exercise social control in the classroom . . .

The ritualistic headteacher is likely to be rather formal in his face-to-face relationships with his staff and pupils, practising a great deal of *social distance.* In many ways he tries to conceal the *self* within his role. Any hint that such a head was fallible and 'human' might detract from his ritualistic authority.

King contrasts 'ritualistic authority' with 'charismatic authority' and it becomes apparent that his classifications have much in common with those of Max Weber:[1] traditional, bureaucratic and charismatic. The terminology used by both writers has suffered from semantic debasement. Bureaucratic has increasingly become a word of derogation. Charismatic, which the two writers employ with slightly different implications, has lost its classical meaning through over-use. King particularly implies that ritual-istic and charismatic leadership are opposites. It is doubtful whether this is true. Both are fundamentally hierarchical, and in their extreme form autocratic; it is seldom that either is encoun-tered in textbook isolation.

King nevertheless does us a service by depicting in ritualism a style of leadership which has long been a potent force in educa-tional management. Its seemingly impeccable pedigree, traced through the great names of nineteenth-century public school headmasters, adds to that potency. It was to these exemplars of leadership that, from the beginning of the nineteenth century, most of the headteachers of state schools consciously or uncon-sciously looked. What is more, contemporary society itself enjoined these examples upon them. Matthew Arnold's influence as an educationist lies more in his respectability and conformity to the social mores of his age and the decades which immediately followed than in the originality of his educational philosophy.

The ritualistic headteacher is obviously most effective in the management structure of the school when the great majority of pupils and their parents willingly accept and conform to his style. For many of the adult generation the organization of the school both reflected and underwrote the organization of their working lives. As will later become apparent, it is not until elements of society for one reason or another begin seriously to challenge the

[1] See page 3.

hierarchical structures which are implicit in this style of leadership, not until the first murmurings of participation are heard in other societal organizations, that the effectiveness of ritualism begins to erode. However, no style of leadership based on hierarchical power – and both ritualistic and charismatic leadership are so based, contrasting though they may appear to be – unresistingly accepts that it has ceased to achieve its objectives.

Certainly it cannot be claimed that ritualism did not meet the needs of prewar secondary schools. In these, both in grammar and in elementary schools, very little participatory structure was evident. With clearly defined educational goals, accepted unquestioningly by society, minimal staff involvement beyond that of teaching 'well' was looked for. In the grammar school 'well' implied pupil success in the General Schools Certificate (five subjects with credit gave exemption from matriculation) and in the Higher School Certificate (where performance at credit level gave exemption from the Intermediate BA). It is likely that few who studied in those prewar grammar schools knew the significance of 'matric' and 'inter'. Most pupils were painfully aware, however, that success provided them, in an era of three million unemployed, with the key to good jobs, the professions, even the university. In prewar Manchester, shop girls in the better department stores required matriculation for employment behind the counter. Today five O levels will take them directly into training for management. The threat of unemployment was as powerful a performance incentive and behavioural control on the teaching staff as on the pupils of the grammar school. Correcting, marking, record-keeping were scrupulous. Punishments were codified, and expected, by both the pupils and the headmaster, to be administered. Excessive punishment was not necessarily a sign of weakness; nor, whatever some may think today, was it immediate evidence of sadism. The despised ones, the failures, the teachers who did not return the following term and whose departure was not announced with suitable expressions of regret and goodwill at the final assembly, could look to no support from within the staffing structure. For there was no staffing structure to look to. There was the headmaster. It would be tautologous to define his role. It was evident in his title. There was the senior master, the day-to-day executive functionary. Finally, there were teachers of greater or less experience, entitled to greater or less reverence within the structure according to length of service, and length of service within the school, in most cases one and the same.

The elementary schools attracted staff of a different calibre. Since, it was argued, anyone could get into a grammar school on a scholarship if he worked hard enough, whatever social class he came from, their task was self-evident: to cope with the failures. One copes with failures by a policy of containment. For the conformists and the achievers – within their limits, needless to say – there was the carrot of a good reference for a job. For others there was the stick. There was little subject specialization. The staff structure was even more clearly defined in that responsibility for each pupil obviously rested with his class teacher. As a consequence that pupil's plus or minus deviation from the expected standard of behaviour and achievement was to the credit or debit of the teacher concerned. Elementary schools followed closely the

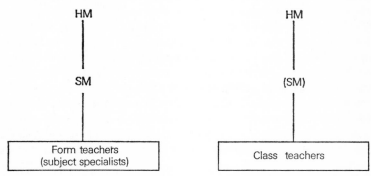

Figure 1. Secondary and elementary school organization

structural pattern of the primary school. Indeed, it is too easily forgotten how few schools, particularly outside the cities, had been reorganized following the Spens Report.[1] Even in 1947, over a million children were receiving instruction in all-age schools: 22 per cent of all children receiving full-time education in England and Wales. By 1952 that percentage had been reduced to 14 per cent, but the number of children in such schools was still over 800 000, because of the rising birthrate. When our first comprehensive schools were opening their doors in London and Birmingham to their school populations of two thousand, when the first questions about educational management were beginning to be raised, there were still 5000 all-age schools in England and Wales.

[1] *Report of the Consultative Committee of the Board of Education on Secondary Education with Special Reference to Grammar Schools and Technical High Schools* (HMSO, 1938).

As can be seen from Figure 1 the management structure of the grammar and elementary or all-age schools was basically identical. The substitution after the implementation of the 1944 Act of the word 'modern' for 'elementary' did nothing to change the structure, though the grouping together of all schools catering for pupils over eleven as 'secondary' ensured that future structural changes affected the tripartite system as a whole.

The effect of Burnham

In the immediate postwar years few responsibility allowances were paid by local education authorities: there was provision in the 1945 Report for above scale allowances to be paid to 14 per cent to 16 per cent of the qualified assistant teachers in the service of the authority, changed to $12\frac{1}{2}$ per cent to $17\frac{1}{2}$ per cent in 1948. There was no obligation on the authority, be it noted, to give these allowances equitably to the schools within its jurisdiction. In 1951, however, 'changes were made in the method of determining the number and value of posts for which special allowances could be paid. The Burnham Report of that year prescribed ranges of total expenditure on allowances which were linked to the unit totals of schools . . . It was left to the discretion of the l.e.a. to determine the number of teachers to receive special allowances and the rates of the allowances to be paid to individual teachers.'[1]

This salary agreement, therefore, was the first to provide the opportunity for the introduction into the structure of middle management. The phrase 'left to the discretion of the l.e.a.' has significant undertones. Often this would imply the extent to which a headteacher could persuade his education officer to accept his proposals for the number of recipients and the amount they were to be paid. The benefits of these discretionary powers depended very largely on the finance committee of the administrative area, county or county borough, city or excepted district in which a school happened to be. For the ranges of total expenditure were very wide. 'For example, for an average sized grammar school' (today probably in group 10) 'the range of expenditure was £821

---

[1] The quotations and much valuable information for these paragraphs were taken from an article by Vivenne Greenhalgh, 'The movement of teachers' salaries 1920–68', *Journal of Educational Administration and History*, Vol. 1, No. 1 (University of Leeds). See also the article by Freda Conway 'Schools teachers' salaries 1945–1959', *The Manchester School of Economical and Social Studies*, Vol. XXX, No. 2.

to £1,219'. This is a very wide margin of discretion! It was further widened by the ability of an authority to make greater or additional allowances where desirable from an 'Area Pool', calculated from a total 'head count' of pupils in the authority's schools – 'four bob a nob', to be precise.

The consequent varying practices – above all the marked differentiation between generous and parsimonious authorities – led the 1956 Burnham Report to introduce 'a scale of allowances for deputy heads and . . . graded posts carrying fixed allowances for teachers undertaking special responsibility, special work of an advanced character, etc.' in addition to four grades of payment for heads of subject departments in schools in which advanced work was undertaken. It is interesting to observe that the role of deputy head was not specifically recognized as fundamental to the structure of schools until this year (1956), though deputy head-ships could be and were established, needless to say, within the range of allowances available in previous reports. This rapid diversification of reward opportunities in education was at one and the same time a reflection of the need for the delegation of responsibility and a considerable incentive towards the stratification of power. There are a number of important organizational side-effects of these decisions on salary. The first is that the size of the secondary school, or to be more precise the number of pupils and their ages, becomes a major factor in determining the staffing structure. The second is that the specification of the roles for which head of department allowances were to be paid (by 1961 a fifth grade, E, had been added) quite clearly established a 'pecking order' among subjects.

There were subjects which, because they did not attract pupils for advanced work, did not qualify for a head of department allowance. There is no doubt that some headteachers, particularly in comprehensive schools, deliberately sought to introduce advanced work in certain subjects to enable them adequately to reward heads of department in these subjects. This may have been no bad thing for those subjects and those teachers; but as an example of sound educational administration it beggars descrip-tion!

More important still, value judgements were made by authority, and consequently within the school, on the contribution of those in academic roles, who qualified for the head of depart-ment allowances, and those in non-academic, usually pastoral roles, who did not. Some years were to pass before this inequity was even eroded. Not until 1971 was it finally eliminated from the salary structure, by the simplification to five scales of pay,[1] with no strings attached. One can by no means feel equally confident that it has been eliminated from the management structures of individual schools.

To sum up, there have been three major determinants in the organization of schools which stem directly from the salary agreements, and for which local education authorities and teachers' associations must share responsibility: the unit total of the school, which is far from the same thing as the size of a school, when a sixth-form pupil may have the 'value' of four first-form pupils; the specification of function, which contributed significantly to the overriding importance attached to curricular as distinct from pastoral roles; and the freedom of headteachers to allocate to posts in school largely identical in size and structure completely different allowances, reflecting either the relative importance in the mind of one individual of a colleague's role, or often the scarcity value of a particular subject in a particular school at a given moment in time. Subjective judgements and expediency rule the day, not principles of management.

The development of secondary-school structures

During the decade following the 1956 Burnham Report, which was also the era of greatest expansion in comprehensive reorganization, in the absence of any significant thinking or writing about educational management, structures began to evolve which were merely an extension of those shown in Figure 1.

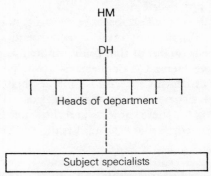

Figure 2. Secondary-school curricular organization

[1] Six, once more, with the introduction the following year of the three, discretionary, senior teacher posts in schools beyond a certain size; and then five again with the amalgamation of scales 2 and 3 under the Burnham agreement which followed the Houghton Report.

The remoteness of the head from the teaching staff became accentuated. At the same time, he became more open to the pressures of subject-based groups and, as the rate of curricular change accelerated, more dependent on his middle-management staff, whether or not he was prepared to admit it. It is difficult to maintain the polymath image in the face of increasingly esoteric departmental language. In many schools interdepartmental frictions grew. After all, specialist heads of department were trained to value their own specializations. It was only natural, where educational resources were limited, for them to do battle for what they valued. Battles require opponents, and they were readily found within the structural peer-group: their 'fellow' departmental heads.

The growth of pastoral structures

Against this curricular structure there had been growing for a number of years a rival, pastoral structure. The house system had existed before the war mainly as a means of facilitating intra-school groupings for sports contests, musical festivals and similar rivalries for cups, colours and other ritualistic insignia. The development of corporate rivalry had been increasingly seized upon in the postwar years as a control system based upon the honour and dishonour of the winning or losing of housepoints. Kinslade School[1] was formed, when in the 1970s comprehensive reorganization finally caught up with this Kemshire market town, from the amalgamation of two single-sex secondary-modern schools. The Jubilee School for Girls, built in 1935, established a reputation with parents and employers as a well-conducted school with high standards. When, after the 1944 Act, it became a secondary-modern school its new headmistress introduced the house system, and herself presented the Nora Fremantle cup for the house annually awarded the most points for good behaviour. A former pupil, now a primary teacher in Kinslade and the mother of a teenage daughter, remembers with embarrassment the

[1] The Kinslade School simulation was devised in 1970 by the author and Dick Ashman, and since then used as the basis for workshop courses in educational management, attended (at the time of writing) by well over 500 headteachers and senior staff. A number of incidents, management structures, techniques and situations have been cast in this book in the Kinslade mould, to give them coherence and credibility. The latter they certainly should have. Every one has a firm foundation of truth – even if some, like that which follows, may seem far-fetched. Only details have been altered to preserve anonymity.

half-hour discussion with her headmistress and housemistress as to whether she could honourably retain her position as house captain, and her self respect, when her name was to be read out at the following Monday's assembly for losing a housepoint because she had forgotten her housecraft apron. To her daughter the story belongs not merely to another generation, but to another world.

Towards the end of the 1950s and particularly in the 1960s, however, pastoral organization entered a new dimension. This is not the place to chart the rapid development of home–school relationships, nor to evaluate the contribution of the house and later the year system to that development. *Pastoral Care*,[1] edited by Michael Marland, in this series, does that. The most important unit of the pastoral system, whether organized on a house or year basis, is the tutor group: thirty pupils of the full range of ability with one teacher as tutor.

Whether the teacher taught his group, or even some of his group was, and remains, of less importance than the daily contact he has with them. Even more important, this contact is one which can rapidly extend to the family, since the tutor is the regular channel of communication over absence, illness, family difficulties and behavioural problems. He maintains continuity of communication, since in most schools the advantage of his moving from year to year with his students became obvious. The tutor group became, as the curricular organization of the school grew more complex, with sets, options and other groupings and regroupings, the one stable unit in the child's school structure. Tutors rapidly developed a role which was in the main understanding, and sometimes over-protective. However, since most teachers must of necessity be tutors, just as once most were form masters and mistresses, it follows that there were among them some who understood the scope of this role less well than others. Certainly it was a step forward from the form system whereby the newest and most inexperienced teacher was frequently allocated 3C. Nevertheless there were many who saw themselves as markers of registers, compilers of reports and punishers of latecomers. Heads, enthusiastic for the possibilities of the new system, wrote house periods into the timetable. Some teachers used these excellently, to check work

[1] Chapter 8, 'Reaching home' by Patrick McGeeney, while recognizing that there are still headteachers 'firmly dug in behind the ramparts of traditional authoritarianism', shows that we have made much progress since his *Parents are Welcome* was published (Longmans, 1969). In Chapter 4, 'Groups and groupings', Michael Marland very fairly balances the arguments for and against house and year, vertical and horizontal pastoral structures.

standards, to promote involvement in school and house affairs and above all to take the opportunity to learn about their group. Others used them as marking periods, while the children did their homework.

Partly to promote good ideas, partly to provide a control upon pastoral staff and pupils, heads appointed housemasters and mistresses. Except in a few schools, they ranked, in the early 1960s, at a status level below most heads of department. The size of a house tended to be larger than appropriate to what we now recognize to be a cohesive and manageable unit. Because four houses lent themselves so evidently to inter-house competition, the tendency was to have three hundred pupils or more in a house. The convenience of, say, two tutor groups a year, possibly merging to one in the pre-RoSLA fifth, outweighed any real consideration of whether a meaningful relationship could be established between as many as twelve members of staff – a senior house teacher and an assistant of opposite sex in a mixed school, and ten tutors – and three hundred children spanning the full secondary age range. For heads, the dilemma lay in the shortage of experienced pastoral staff and the regrettable tendency of school entries to fluctuate, sometimes according to local conditions, more often according to the vagaries of l.e.a. policy. Today it is widely held – though not so widely practised – that the maximum effective pastoral unit is 120. There is a growing belief, stimulated doubtless by the advent of sixth-form colleges in some l.e.a. areas, that the school sixth form should be encouraged to regard itself as a homogeneous social unit, not divided on a house basis. In some schools a compromise is reached, with sixth-form students voluntarily contributing to their former houses as aides to the staff in charge of units of younger pupils. For those planning to teach, to do social work, or otherwise to concern themselves with people, the benefits of a more adult role as assistant tutors, sports coaches and the like has a greater appeal than the enforced infantilism of belonging to the blues, the reds, the yellows or the greens.

The introduction of mixed-ability teaching in the earlier secondary years removed the greatest obstacle to the cohesiveness of the house tutor group. Dual loyalties, friendship patterns within two structures are confusing and disturbing to young secondary children probably meeting the specialized school day for the first time. If pupils are taught wholly or mainly in tutor groups the dichotomy disappears. There was, however, in the minds of many educationists a confusion of objectives. How important did the homogeneity of the group rank against the attainment of educational standards? Was mixed-ability teaching by tutor groups an enforcement of egalitarianism, wrongly ascribed by opponents of the comprehensive school as a basic tenet? Or would mixed-ability teaching prove with adequate preparation so to provide for differing abilities as to make compartmentalization into ability groups wasteful of human resources and self-perpetuating? The debate continues. Indeed, until recently it seemed that it would be both pointless and endless, since the effect of teaching in mixed-ability groups compared with streamed groups looked to be only marginally more measurable than the advantages and disadvantages of the social mix within the pastoral group.

Banbury School is so far unique in this country. It is a 'federal grouping of the seven school communities which together offer a complete range of secondary education for Banbury and some neighbouring villages of North Oxfordshire'.[1] The school communities relevant to what follows are the four Halls of the Lower School (11 to 15) and the Upper School (16 to 19). The terms of reference of what is known as the Banbury Project were 'to examine the differences, social and academic which arise in the early years of secondary education from two systems of ability grouping, homogeneous and heterogeneous, within a single controlled situation'. David Newbold was appointed research officer to the project, the first entirely school-based project to be supported by the Department of Education and Science.

The Halls are largely independent within the federal structure, but it is possible 'to have matched intakes from the same primary schools entering different Halls, taught on a common curriculum, but organized into several types of ability grouping'. The project proper began with the 1972 intake, what it calls the *definitive cohort*, after a year's experience of a *trial cohort*. Full results cannot therefore be expected until 1977, when the former will have completed statutory secondary schooling. Preliminary findings are nevertheless illuminating: 'in the 11 to 13 age range the relative effects of the different systems of ability grouping on academic progress are small in comparison with other factors'.

It is already becoming apparent that the importance of the project may lie less in any conclusive indication that either form of grouping is 'better' (whatever that may mean) but in the highlighting of the vital relationship between school organization and educational management. In short, a school will still have to decide upon its organizational structure, and seek to make it work.

[1] This and subsequent quotations on the Banbury Project are from *The School as a Centre of Enquiry* (Pubansco, 1975).

House system or year system?

Ten years ago the house organization was paramount. Since then the year organization has rapidly gained popularity, and in reorganized schools is almost certainly predominant.[1] The differences are largely irrelevant, since the tutor group is the essential basis of both. The year structure suits the larger school, the school with inequalities of numbers on roll in succeeding years, and the school which is less concerned about maintaining inter-unit rivalries. Some heads have deliberately cultivated the year system to counteract what they regard as a dangerous conformity to competitive rather than collaborative principles; others have simply found it more suitable to the structure of their schools or the circumstances of expansion brought about by reorganization. The house structure is shown in Figure 3.

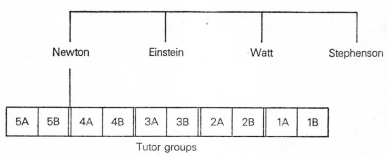

Figure 3. House structure: eight-form-entry school

The house structure has the apparent merit of permanence, but the merit disappears once it is recognized that it may be a permanence of inferiority to the other houses. The dependence upon the initiative of the housemaster or mistress is considerable. In the eight-form-entry school taken as the model for Figure 3 the size of the group is excessive, particularly in view of the age range within the group. A traditional view is that the house system promotes qualities of leadership in the oldest pupils. A cynic might be heard to observe 'leadership to what end?' In a weak house, bullying and antisocial behaviour may come from the top; in any house system there is a tendency to make the young seem even younger.

[1] In a random sample of fifteen East Anglian schools, twelve were organized on a year basis and only three on a house basis.

The eight-form-entry mixed school may be forced to a four-house structure of 300 pupils by the ostensible need for both a housemaster and mistress, since the pastoral advice of a member of the same sex as the pupil is generally regarded as important. I believe this to be another myth. Indeed the greater value of having a member of each sex in a pastoral role is, in my experience, that boys have a mother figure to turn to and girls a father figure! One of the best women teachers I ever knew could reduce a strapping six footer to the edge of tears with 'Well, Steven, you have disappointed me. I never dreamt that a man like you could behave in such a way.' And girls approached her teacher husband freely to seek advice about the most intimate details of their love life.

An eight-house structure is likely to create too many groups for the establishment of a common ethos among groups; a four-house structure, too large a unit for a common ethos within the group. The year structure in a school of this size has therefore organizationally much to commend it. Here the year may split into two half-year divisions of 120 pupils (Figure 4).

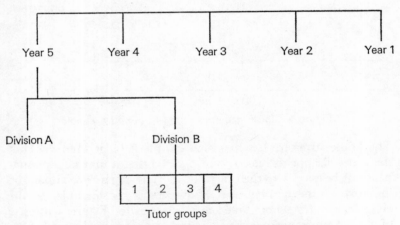

Figure 4. Year structure: eight-form-entry school

Or two years may divide into four divisions with sixty from each year. The latter system combines an element of continuity with an element of change. In an 11 to 16 school it probably forces the fifth year out of the system, but there is merit in that too, since these pupils need special consideration in the year in which most will take examinations and all will need final preparation for careers or continued education.

Most important of all, the year system allows for the introduction of a more senior level of management: the year tutor with responsibility for, in the eight-form-entry model, 240 pupils; or the lower (etc.) school tutor with responsibility for 480 pupils, possibly with the assistance of a senior member of staff of the other sex.

To sum up: the house system requires eight senior pastoral staff, each of whom has responsibility for 150 pupils; the year system requires ten pastoral staff each responsible for 120 pupils, supported by three to five year staff. The 'cost' in terms of posts of responsibility is obviously greater in the year system; but the existence of three tiers of support (tutor, division tutor and year tutor), as against two (tutor and housemaster/mistress), may well make the cost worth while. It is a good rule-of-thumb measure that the 'expenditure' of points on pastoral posts of responsibility should be half that on curricular posts of responsibility. The more expensive system will still fall within that proportion.

A pastoral system is of necessity pyramidal since the greater the support that any child needs, the greater the expertise required to give it. Certainly the pyramid should be broadly based. The role of the tutor should be as extensive as he is prepared to make it in respect of the child and his family. However, when the aid of outside agencies is required there must be movement towards the apex of the pyramid, if we are not to produce a ridiculous fragmentation of effort. An untenable situation would be created if each tutor dealt directly with the educational welfare officer over suspected truancies or cases of need. These must be channelled through more senior members of staff. The decision when to seek the assistance of an understaffed family guidance clinic cannot be left to the individual tutor. He needs to discuss the case with his senior colleagues so that an informed assessment of the situation is reached. Nevertheless, the key to decision-making on pastoral matters is undoubtedly the tutor, and any tendency to bypass him vitiates his role. Case-study conferences on particularly difficult behavioural problems are very valuable both in enabling a common policy towards the child to be evolved, particularly between curricular and pastoral staff, and to provide the material for in-service education of staff. All the college lectures, all the instructions in the handbook for staff will be of little direct avail in a given situation of gross indiscipline or serious maladjustment. It is in case conferences that differing ideologies may become reconciled, or at least tolerated, and the power of some children to manipulate staff exposed and minimized.

The expansion of departmental structures

At the same time as a pastoral system was evolving in our secondary schools, several curriculum developments were beginning to cast shadows across the clearly defined structure of departmental responsibility. In a streamed structure, the main dialogue between one departmental head and his peers was over the transfer up or down of pupils who were succeeding or failing in his particular subject. Streaming is now widely recognized as a self-proving system[1] – children in the main live up to teacher expectation and so prove streaming, like selection, 'right' – and arguments were rare. There were always a few children whose transfer could be readily agreed (remembering that 'ups' must be balanced by 'downs' so that the class sizes should not change) and termly and examination orders of merit easily identified these. There were a few with markedly observable imbalance between, say, mathematical and linguistic ability and it was over these that warfare raged or horse-trading was engaged upon in end-of-term staff meetings.

Streaming in three-form secondary-modern schools like Kinslade's Jubilee School for Girls and Ladysmith Road (Boys) had not seemed particularly rigid: each form represented a quartile of the entire ability range since the first quartile was already in selective schools. With a ten-form-entry comprehensive school, however (and the earliest urban schools were of this or larger size), streaming into deciles soon becomes a patent absurdity. Broad-banding soon began to replace A to Z streaming, usually in three broad bands and remedial classes.

The new system actually *reduced* contact between one department and another. Overlap between one broad band and its neighbour made transfer less necessary. When transfers were proposed, arguments about them were, for the same reason, less heated. In any case, in the large school, transfer decisions might well be the responsibility of staff senior to departmental heads – the head of lower school, for example. He would, it was held, be impartial, and able to make judgements on criteria additional to academic attainment, based upon his knowledge of a child's motivation, health or attendance record.

[1] See Brian Jackson, *Streaming: an Education System in Miniature* (Routledge & Kegan Paul, 1964) for evidence of this in primary schools; and E. Ferri, *Streaming: Two Years Later* (N.F.E.R., 1971).

In these larger schools *intra*departmental activity grew,[1] as syllabuses were developed appropriate to each band, and heads of department hammered out with their colleagues reading lists for the semi-literate teenager, or methods of teaching modern languages to those below the top quartile (pupils who in the tripartite system rarely had opportunities to study such subjects), or practical courses in the crafts for those with limited theoretical abilities. In many ways this parochialism was a necessary precursor to the *inter*departmental activity which was to follow.

It would be absurd to pretend that one can now detect a planned progression in educational objectives. For one thing, secondary reorganization in this country has been so extenuated, so fraught with anxiety and so variable between one authority and another, that few schools were able, in the late 1950s and early 1960s, to claim much objectivity in their planning. Many were content merely to survive. There were, however, two major educational developments which were significantly to promote a greater dialogue within the school's curricular structure.

In both comprehensive schools and modern schools the early syllabus planning for those pupils without the traditional achievement incentives of the grammar-school pupils led to a growing demand for a similar form of recognition. Some teachers began to advocate school leavers' certificates, and the need first to debate the feasibility of such proposals and then to establish assessment criteria led to a growing purposeful relationship across departmental barriers within the school. In some areas, the local education authorities responded centrally to this demand, and teachers in a variety of disciplines began to collaborate as representatives of their schools in working out the framework of such certificates, and inevitably at the same time creating the climate for an increasing mutual understanding of the objectives of other school departments. Other schools and l.e.a.s began similarly to investigate the opportunities offered by existing examination bodies other than the G.C.E. boards. Some of these had syllabuses already in existence which, while not necessarily what the schools ideally wanted, at least provided the motivation they asked for. Other bodies, traditionally geared to the needs of technical institutions, were prepared to meet the needs of secondary schools if the demand was sufficient to make the exercise economically viable. It is a matter of history that it was this growing demand, not any widespread revolution in educational thinking, that led to the

[1] See Michael Marland, *Head of Department*, in this series (Heinemann, 1971).

setting up of a committee[1] charged with the task of investigating the feasibility of an examination with national validity for pupils in the three (later four) deciles of the ability range below the top 20 per cent. In the mid-1960s, the Beloe baby, the examination for the Certificate of Secondary Education, was in various stages of gestation up and down the land.

The late 1950s and early 1960s saw the development of roles of increasing importance for those charged with curricular responsibility, and with it a perception of increasing interrelationships. Interestingly, while this was happening mainly for the benefit of the 13- to 16-year-old pupils in our schools, another development, far more controversial and decidedly based upon educational ideology rather than consumer demand, was taking place in the interests, it was argued, of younger pupils, primary as well as secondary.

Non-streaming, or mixed-ability grouping, had long been the general practice in our infant schools. Gradually it worked its way into junior schools, particularly those in areas served by comprehensive schools where the need to differentiate between the 'scholarship' class and the also-rans had no further justification. Before long some comprehensive schools, usually those which were already broad-banded, began to wonder whether they might not, in their first year, or perhaps even their first two years, introduce mixed-ability teaching, though with adequate protection for the least able.

What happened in Lawrence Weston School, Bristol, at that time, illustrates the effect that consideration of this major policy change, let alone its implementation, had upon interdepartmental relationships.[2] In 1965 the headmaster decided with his deputy head and senior master that they ought to look into the possible advantages of the mixed-ability teaching that had long been established in a nearby primary school and which, so they had heard and read, was being tried in certain secondary schools. In the next few months they gathered and assessed such evidence as existed, both in print and in practice. They then put their ideas to the heads of department and proposed a series of meetings in which they would collectively evaluate the possibilities of intro-

---

[1] The committee's findings, published as *Secondary School Examinations other than the GCE* (H.M.S.O., 1960), is generally known as the Beloe Report, after its chairman Robert Beloe.

[2] Compare Michael Tucker's account of 'Organisational Change: the Process of Unstreaming' in M. G. Hughes, *Secondary School Administration: A Management Approach* (Pergamon, 1970).

ducing this major innovation. These meetings took place over six months, with departmental, interdepartmental and full staff discussions. They decided finally that they would introduce mixed-ability grouping in the following September, giving all departments eight months to prepare new schemes of work. After six months of experience they would take one of three measures. If they regarded the experiment as a failure they would abandon it the next September. If it was judged successful they would either retain it for all future first years, or expand it to cover the first two years. The mathematics and languages departments, while sympathetic to the general principle, felt themselves unable to cope with the techniques of mixed-ability teaching and for these setting was introduced. Practical subjects wished to work with mixed-ability grouping for all pupils in the year, based on their pastoral tutor groups. Other subjects required a structure which permitted the withdrawal of children needing remedial education. Major innovations of this kind radically affect the management structure of a school, whether it is aware of the fact or not. Imperceptibly a number of self-contained departments were propelled

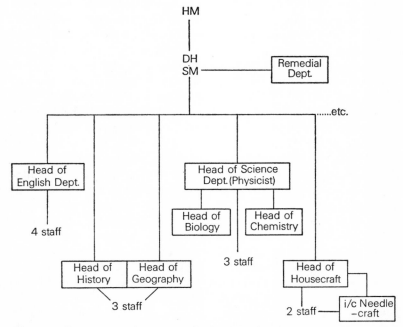

Figure 5. Departmental structure (1967–68) of a six- to seven-form-entry comprehensive school

by common objectives into a relationship that nobody could have anticipated. There grew an awareness that the thinking in one area of the curriculum might provide the solution to the problem arising in another area. Techniques were shared, mutual criticism became acceptable. This school was, for the first time, beginning to systematize management skills. Diagrammatically the departmental structure was evolving as shown in Figure 5.

There remained, however, two weaknesses in the structure. First, the fragmentation into a large number of departments made curricular innovation and evaluation a long drawn out and sometimes fratricidal business. Secondly, the structure retained a hierarchical form, one likely to perpetuate the idea that change, however democratically discussed, came from the top downwards. The management system, in other words, reflected the systems prevalent in the world of industry and commerce in this country.

Larger units with greater responsibility

One of the lessons of modern warfare is that independent units, guerrilla or commando, with training develop an ability in decision-making far beyond their presumed capacities. Like children in streamed situations, adults too perform according to expectation. Perhaps school management systems were being structured on too limited an expectation of the capacity of those whom we now call middle-management staff. Was it possible to move schools away from the traditional pyramidal structures of management? It was a commonplace observation that large schools had within their ranks those who would have held higher positions, and accordingly exercised greater powers of decision-making, had they been in smaller schools. What kind of structure would give such people great autonomy without destroying the unity of purpose of the school? The answer, for the curricular structure of the school at least, seemed to lie in the principle of 'federal decentralization'.[1] The number of units in such a system which can adhere to a common policy – indeed which can contribute to the formulation of a common policy – is considerably smaller than the number of departments, usually from fourteen to eighteen, which had grown up in most comprehensive schools. The faculty system, in which a number of related subjects were grouped together, increasingly found favour in the organization of large secondary schools. A typical grouping might be:

[1] See Peter Drucker, *The Effective Executive* (Harper & Row, 1966).

1. *Humanities* – combining history, geography, economics, sociology, environmental studies, religious education
2. *Mathematics and Science*
3. *Creative-expressive* – combining literature, music, dance, drama and physical education
4. *Design and Technology* – combining art and craft, needle-craft, technical drawing, woodwork and metalwork, engineering
5. *Home Economics*
6. *Languages*

The number of faculties and the 'subjects' they combine are of far less importance than the principle.[1] The physical structure of the school, the presence of staff with particular predilections, even the opportunities afforded by the environment of the school may all affect the composition of the model. Within each faculty, if it is of any size, there is likely to be a substructure. If this substructure is nothing more than a grouping together of departments under departmental heads, little has been achieved in the new organization. The substructure is best depicted in overlapping areas of commitment as in Figure 6.

Where areas overlap, responsibility lies in both sectors. Ideally,

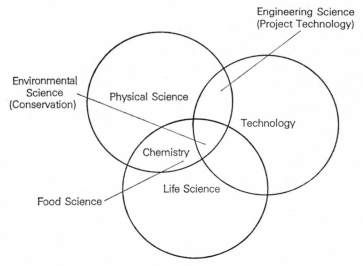

Figure 6. Model of a Faculty of Science and Technology

[1] The faculty and departmental structures of a number of secondary schools are given in Appendix 1.

the head of faculty and his specialist assistants form a faculty management team. If watertight departments have been replaced by watertight faculties, again we have achieved very little. The expectations for the substructures are no less applicable to the faculties themselves. Unless there are overlapping areas of commitment between faculties, and unless heads of faculties regard themselves primarily as a curriculum management team, we will have decentralization, but not federal decentralization.

The absence from the model of any link with the headteacher or his deputies is deliberate, but should not be taken to indicate that they have abdicated all responsibility, or removed to an ivory tower where they dream educational ideals. Nevertheless, federal decentralization applied to education casts the head and his deputies in a role totally different from that of tradition. To nobody will this apply more than to the deputy. In his M.A.(Ed) thesis Peter Burnham sought to evaluate the role of the deputy head. In his research in a number of schools he could find little common ground and even less role definition. In Chapter 3 I quote from a fourteen-point definition of the role of a deputy head prepared by a headmaster for the information of candidates. In many schools the last point is both first and last: 'To carry out such other duties as the Headmaster may reasonably require.' In his eminently readable chapter on the role of the deputy head in *Headship in the 1970s*, Burnham heads one section 'the man-in-the-middle role conflict hypothesis'. It is an apt description of the limbo in which many deputies have lived.

The chapters which follow show a number of ways in which deputy heads and other members of staff – and indeed the headteacher himself – become integral parts, with clearly assigned roles, in the consultative and executive structure of the school.

3 Role definition and evaluation

The worker in industry has a task that can be clearly and specifically defined. His job is to make that, assemble this, spray the other. To ensure that the finished product is of a satisfactory standard, inspectors or quality controllers sample or check the material outcome of the worker's performance. Many of the tasks of the worker in industry call for skills of a very high level, scientific or technical knowledge worthy of respect in any society which dignifies labour. Nevertheless, what he does is done to material things and inanimate objects, even though as in the motor vehicle industry the lives of fellow human beings who use his product depend upon his skills, or as in coalmining the lives of his workmates depend upon the skill with which he handles the machinery he uses or the coal he produces.

In any industry it is possible to analyse the requirements of a particular task, and to define it precisely. Increasingly, this has led to the division of a task into a number of sub-tasks, and the allocation of sub-tasks to individuals who can become more and more highly specialized, and therefore more accurate, more speedy and more cost-effective. Experts in organization and method examine in minute detail the performance of each sub-task and find ways in which the movements of the worker may be reduced or the positioning of his machine or tools may be improved to accelerate still further his productivity. Eventually there arises the possibility that these sub-tasks have become so defined that they no longer need men to perform them. A machine, the computer, directs the machines. The role of the industrial worker becomes, in an instant, revolutionized. Manual dexterities must be replaced by organizational skills. The man unable to adapt to his new role is no longer required. The man who succeeds in adaptation acquires a new status. Nevertheless, however changed the role, it is still clearly defined.

How usefully can we apply the precision of industrial role definition to a service organization like a school or a hospital? At first sight they are poles apart. Schools and hospitals are primarily concerned with people not with materials. They are staffed by people with dedication, who are inclined to talk of their vocation – literally that to which they were 'called' – rather than their job. There is a remarkably close relationship between the client (the pupil and the patient) and the staff. Schools, indeed, have a secondary clientele, the parent and the employer. Though both schools and hospitals are accountable, they are generally called to account only after something has gone disastrously wrong. A school, and a hospital, will resist evaluation against other schools and hospitals on the grounds that there are too many imponderables to permit valid objective assessments to be made. But here the comparison ends. Hospital workers, from porters to registrars, have clearly delineated role definitions. School workers do not. To be more precise, school ancillaries – cleaners, caretakers, clerical assistants – do. But teachers, who constitute the majority of those who work in schools (for financial reward, that is!), and whose roles cover a far wider range than those of ancillaries, do so only rarely. Is this because the teacher's role is impossible to define, or because he is highly resistant to attempts to define it?

The need for role definition

The teacher's role *is* capable of definition. In the complex structures of our secondary schools that definition is necessary, if each of us is ever to walk his way through the maze of priorities. The first value of role definition is the apportionment of responsibility. In the pastoral system of a school, for instance, the tutor needs to know clearly the extent of his responsibilities. Obviously he will call the register, receive absence notes and perform a number of routine duties that each school finds no difficulty in listing. But is he, for example, to have responsibility for the work standards of the pupils in his tutorial groups? If so, to what extent? This he must know, for two reasons. In the first place, it is not a responsibility which can be left to chance. Someone must be responsible for each pupil's work standards, if we are to commend the conscientious, and identify the under-achiever. If it is not defined as being within the role of any member of staff, or defined so vaguely that it becomes a meaningless allocation of responsibility, then there will be those tutors who take on this responsibility because they see it as their role, and those who do not. The school as an institution becomes weakened in its sense of purpose. Secondly, the allocation of this role has implications on the relationships between staff, which need to be foreseen and for which management procedures and, even more important, professional attitudes must be developed. The tutor's students will usually fall into three categories: those who are achieving at or beyond expectation; those who are achieving uniformly or widely below expectation; and those who are achieving satisfactorily except in, perhaps, one subject. There are many reasons why children may fall into this last group. The teacher of that subject may be performing inadequately, either through inability to control a class, or through poor preparation or pedagogic skills. The subject teacher's expectation of achievement for the class as a whole or for a particular student may be misconceived. Or the relationship between that particular teacher and that particular pupil may be intervening in the learning process. In any of these situations, what is the tutor's role? What are the limits of his tutorial responsibility to his student and what happens if, in discharging it as he sees it, he oversteps the bounds of what other staff regard as his role?

It is not the answers to these questions which are important to us in considering the management of schools. Two schools may provide totally different answers, according to the management structures each has devised, and yet be equally well managed. It is knowing where one stands which matters most. Moreover, all that has been written about the tutor's role might equally have been written about the subject teacher's role. A century ago this was defined absolutely; but we have moved a long way from the precision of the model lesson, the surveillance of the master of method, the constraints of the formal syllabus. Today's greater freedoms of choice, however desirable, make the apportionment of responsibility even more essential if we are not to founder in a morass of good intentions and personal idiosyncrasies.

The apportionment of responsibility inevitably implies the delineation of relationship. Within any management structure each individual must know to whom and how to refer at the stage when he reaches the limit of his own role definition. This does not imply a highly stratified structure, because roles in an occupation such as teaching have a marked overlap. In a good management system this overlap can be exploited to encourage initiative or to support those in difficulty. In a bad management system it will give rise to abdication from responsibility, 'passing the buck.' The sum total of role definitions within an institution must cover the function of that institution. Put another way, it is the responsibility of the headteacher to see that there are no gaps in his management structure, no situations in which one teacher looks at another and says 'It's not my fault. I didn't know that was my job.'

There are obvious dangers in role definition in an occupation so involved with the vagaries of human nature as the running of a school. The very word 'definition' implies a need to quantify and circumscribe; and we are dealing with people and ideas, not materials and easily identifiable goals. There is the danger too that in defining the role we may be cutting the individual down to too small a size. Room must be left for the role to adapt to the individual. A head of faculty may, for example, be a brilliant innovator but a poor administrator. In his role as innovator he may valuably exceed his brief and act as a stimulus to other curriculum leaders. Are we to rein him in, and direct his attention to the shortcomings of his administration?

Definition without constraints

The headteacher who wants a well managed school will approach role definition by first identifying all the major areas of responsibility. It will become evident that a number of tasks are inter-related, and that he needs to recognize this relationship in assigning them. He knows that the precise cut-off point at which the role of one member of staff ends and that of another begins is difficult to specify. He appreciates that the demands or relative importance of tasks will be inconstant. There will be times of the year when certain tasks make fewer demands on the member of staff concerned; there will be periods of stability or consolidation, and periods of searching and time-consuming change; and there will be times when an outside constraint or impetus reigns in or promotes a particular activity.

It is too often assumed that role definitions in education, following the mechanistic model of most industrial concerns, are unitary. They need not be. Educational management is ideally suited to team management structures. Where there is team responsibility there can be team roles. It is possible to construct a role definition for a head of faculty and his middle-management staff, for example, which leaves freedom for the allocation of specific tasks to the individuals best suited to discharge them.

On the facing page is the list of tasks of the executive team[1] of Kinslade School:

[1] Here, the headteacher and his deputies. A more detailed exposition of the role in educational management of the executive team appears on p. 78.

Curricular

Overall responsibility for co-ordination of curriculum; curriculum development projects; Mode 3 syllabuses; secretary/convenor of Curriculum Development Committee

Overall responsibility for use of educational resources (CCTV, audio-visual equipment, library as resource area, etc.)

Timetable planning; timetable and room changes; supply, part-time and temporary staff

In-service education of staff (circulation of research and discussion material, responsibility for curriculum working parties, staff courses, visits, secondments; liaison with teachers' centre; probationary staff)

Promotion of curriculum bridging groups with staff of feeder schools

Examinations secretary, C.S.E. and G.C.E.

Staff allocation and finance budgeting.

Pastoral

Responsibility for effective working of pastoral structure; secretary/convenor of Pastoral Care Committee

Co-ordination of work of year tutors and their division tutors

Careers guidance programmes

School and leavers' reports; parents' evenings

Organization and planning of subject choice by pupils

Liaison with other school in community, particularly feeder schools

Liaison with social and welfare agencies, police, magistrates' court, industry and commerce

School visits, journeys and exchanges

Overall responsibility for disadvantaged pupils: backward and retarded; maladjusted; physically and emotionally handicapped

Home/school links.

Communal

Liaison with departments and colleges of education; timetabling and supervision of student teachers

Visitors, visiting courses, etc.

Staff welfare

Aesthetics and general care of school buildings and grounds

Extended day activities and youth work

Formal (P.T.A.) and informal parental involvement in school activities

Links with community service organizations

Support for school and community cultural and recreational activities.

It would be easy to assume that the three areas of responsibility, curricular, pastoral and communal, fall neatly one each into the laps of the two deputies and the senior master/mistress. There would be a number of serious disadvantages to such planning, however. It would accentuate the divisions that have traditionally existed in our schools between, in particular, curricular and pastoral responsibility. Associating one member of the executive team in the minds of the staff with one zone of responsibility militates against the concept of collective responsibility within the team as a whole. In the absence of one member of the team, his area of responsibility is more likely to be assumed by another member of the team if the latter is already familiar with some part of it. Understanding of the complexity and interlocking of the areas of responsibility engenders in the executive team a respect for each other's performance, and in the staff as a whole an appreciation of the breadth of their role. Finally, a practical point argued by the members of this executive team themselves: their promotion prospects are bound to be enhanced by their versatility rather than by specialization, since heads are expected to function equally well in all areas!

Michael Marland[1] gives at the departmental level a classic example of the structural weakness in the organization that is implicit in the failure to allocate roles worthy of the incumbents:

> One Head of Department in a large comprehensive school, when questioned at the end of a talk in which he explained his work, was asked, 'What, then, are the duties of your Deputy?' 'Oh', was the answer, 'he is really my secretary.'

There is no recognition in the assignment of roles like this of the basic human need to develop oneself through experience into a role both more extensive and more satisfying. If the deputy head of department were unfit to participate in decision-making areas of responsibility he should not be deputy; but if he were fit, he should not be assigned the role of secretary. This incident is related in a chapter entitled 'The complementary team', and the author concludes the paragraph with this useful aphorism: 'I should offer as a guiding principle . . . "No chores without ideas." '

A role definition is not a list of duties. That there are duties implicit in a role definition nobody would deny. It is when the so-called role definition consists wholly or mainly of a list of duties that we begin to perceive that we are in the presence of a management structure which calls for little initiative, holds the promotion

[1] Michael Marland, *Head of Department* in this series.

of new ideas in low regard, requires conformity and is manifestly hierarchical: in other words, a strongly mechanistic organization.

The details sent to applicants for the post of deputy head in a large comprehensive school[1] consisted, apart from some details of the school and catchment area, entirely of a list.

Deputy Head Teacher (Pastoral)

1. To assist and advise the headmaster in all questions of school policy, organization and staffing.
2. To take charge of the school as and when required by the headmaster.
3. To be responsible for the organization of school functions.
4. To arrange staff supervision duty rotas.
5. To have control of general discipline.
6. To be responsible for compilation of confidential reports as requested by the headmaster.
7. To be responsible for the organization and supervision at morning assembly.
8. To be responsible for the organization and supervision of pupils during the midday lunch period.
9. To assist during the opening of the school day, at other intervals and at the departure of pupils at the close of the day.
10. To be responsible for school fund-raising activities.

With this example, one of many such, I regret to say, that I have come across, I would like the reader to contrast the one that follows. It is succinct, it gives ample scope for the holder of the post to work without feeling that someone is breathing down his neck, it specifies the areas in the management structure to which he must at times refer (and by implication on occasions defer) and, not least in importance, its wording makes clear that this is a humane institution, serious in purpose, but not so serious that it cannot laugh at itself.

The Senior Tutor

The senior tutor (probably not very aptly named) has the crucial task of supervising the day-to-day working of the school timetable. He will:

1. Deploy supply teachers or regular staff to cover classes in the case of staff absence.
2. Advise the senior management team on the practicability from a timetable point of view of releasing staff for expeditions, etc.
3. Assist the planning of the curriculum by advising the academic

[1] The school must of course remain anonymous. I have modified the wording slightly to preserve this anonymity, and I have made a selection from the fourteen duties required of the successful applicant. Yes, this *is* the post referred to in Chapter 2. Duty number 14: *To carry out such other duties as the Headmaster may reasonably require!*

committee of the constraints placed on curriculum development
by practical timetabling considerations.

Perhaps it would be honest if a little brutal to add that the senior
tutor is responsible to the principal for ensuring that all teaching
groups (and staff) are where the timetable says they are, promptly
and in good order.

For the management of a school, role definition has a value far
beyond the immediate and obvious one. In drawing up role definitions, attention is directed to vague generalizations, to areas of
responsibility which have not been covered, or not adequately
covered, to duplication of effort, to gross inequalities of burden,
to unnecessary constraints on initiative.

The aims of any school, because they are philosophical and
idealistic, can all too easily become divorced from reality. Alternatively the immediacy and enormity of the reality can often obscure
the aims. 'It's enough to keep going, without having to think
where!' is a sentiment that few teachers will admit to, but one
none the less that is from time to time implicit in their behaviour.
Clearly to understand one's function within the organization
assists in the translation of aims into objectives. Nor is it only one's
own function that role definition should help one to identify. For
a social group that, within the institution at least, appears to be
very tightly knit and coherent, teachers are often remarkably
isolated. The outsider would scarcely believe how frequently
teachers within one school, and not necessarily a very large one,
disclaim all knowledge of the roles of other members of staff.
Instead of seeking to close this gap by enquiry, they may even
cocoon themselves within their own immediate tasks. Role definitions should not be known only by the head and the holder of a
particular responsibility. The whole pattern of role definitions,
which constitutes the management structure of the school, should
be common currency. This leaves every member of staff wide
open to criticism. It also exposes whether the objectives that are
the stepping stones to the institution's aims are realizable, and
whether the tactics being adopted towards a particular end are
part of the overall strategy, or merely expedients. For only through
the *performance* of staff can the gap between theory and practice
be closed. This exposure is good, where there is a sense of security.
Security grows from mutual reliance.

Evaluation of performance

Role definition encourages self-realization and self-assessment. It
gives rise, in fact, to two levels of personal assessment. The first is

simply this: 'To what extent am I achieving my role objectives?' The second level is deeper, and even more important to the school and the individual, since it is prognostic of future development: 'To what extent have I become, or recognized that I cannot become, the type of person able to achieve my present role objectives? Have I the capacity to extend my role?' So far I have gone no further than to indicate the possibilities of self-assessment. What of external assessment? The role definition provides the measuring rod. Who is to do the measuring? This is a task to which we constantly close our eyes and our minds in the management of schools. No industry could afford to ignore the measurement of performance and potential as we do in education. There is only one such assessment incumbent on us in the teaching profession: the reports that decide that a teacher has, or has not successfully completed his probation period. Even these reports are usually structured by the local education authority in the loosest way imaginable, with little guidance to the head as to what questions he should be asking himself in assessing the probationer. Thereafter there is no required evaluation for the next forty years or more, unless an inspector should happen to remark 'How's Mr X getting on then?' or unless a teacher applies for a post elsewhere. This eventuality is dealt with more fully in Chapter 4.

Should there not be periodic assessments of the way in which each member of staff, *including the headteacher*, is attaining his role objectives? Certainly this happens in most other countries. I am indebted to an American visitor to my school for this account of the procedure set up in his community college. 'The purpose of evaluation of instruction'[1] it begins 'should be to increase the instructor's awareness of education methods, problems and goals, and to further his ability to improve himself and his classes.' The instructor meets his department chairman in his first month of service to discuss and to develop 'a mutually acceptable evaluation program'. The evaluation procedure will include at least three of these elements:

1. summary of student evaluation;
2. peer evaluation;
3. classroom visitation;
4. self-evaluation.

[1] We should not allow the words *instruction* and *instructor*, nor the fact that American teachers are subject, as we are not, to the threat of termination of contract, to deter us from seeing the positive values in the scheme. It is worth observing that it was drawn up with the co-operation and full agreement of the 'instructors' themselves.

The criteria for evaluation must include:
1. general effectiveness of instruction –
   (a) competence in subject matter;
   (b) clarity and interest in presentation;
2. general effectiveness in student advising.'

It may include a number of extra-departmental activities – among them, interestingly, professional writings and research. The director maintains a file on each instructor which contains all the material on which evaluation is based. There are two copies of every document, the original file copy requiring the signature of the instructor, and a second copy which is held by the instructor. The departmental evaluation committee consists of three members, one of whom is of the instructor's choosing. This committee will discuss with the instructor the results of the evaluation procedures previously agreed upon and prepare a written recommendation. The account continues with the procedures when there is a negative evaluation. The rights of the individual are fully protected, and spelled out in detail. As soon as the teacher is on 'continuous appointment', evaluation is triennial. Such a system could, improperly handled, become fratricidal, nepotistic, even open to corrupt practices. Properly conducted, with full safeguards, it might lead to an increased acceptance of personal and collective responsibility, which is one of the main themes of this book. If we are not ready, as the teachers in this American school patently are, to submit our teaching abilities to periodic reappraisal, at least we ought to be able to clarify within the school the procedure and criteria for the evaluation of probationer teachers.

It is not merely that in many schools the probationer teacher does not know *how* his performance is being evaluated. All too often he does not know *by whom* it is being evaluated. I heard one teacher, now in middle management, say that he knew as a student, vaguely, that there was something called a probationary year, but that when he began teaching the first and only occasion he heard of it officially was when he received a letter from the l.e.a. saying that he had successfully completed it. In this case, an exceptional situation one hopes, the headteacher seems to have completely abdicated from his responsibilities for that important aspect of that young teacher's early in-service education: assessment of progress.

If G. E. Whalley's survey[1] of 1500 secondary teachers working

[1] *Teacher-Education from the Teachers' Point of View*, University of Leeds Institute of Education Colleges Curriculum Project (April 1974).

in schools in a particular locality is representative of the general opinion of the profession (and there is no reason to suppose that it is not) then 65 per cent hold the view that responsibility for the supervision and guidance of probationary teachers should lie with the school *alone*. A further 26 per cent saw it as being the concern of the school in conjunction with a local college of education and/or the county inspectorate. This may be a *faute de mieux* observation. As the report observes: 'Possibly this is because many teachers see a clear distinction between initial training and the purpose and work of the probation year. Perhaps some regard the colleges as lacking in the necessary knowledge and expertise.'

However, before schools begin to preen themselves on *their* expertise it would be salutary for them to learn that 60 per cent of secondary teachers regard the guidance and supervision given to probationers as insufficient. One may reasonably conclude that it is widely felt that it is the school's role to give this support, but that it is inadequately discharging this function.

The role of the school only becomes manifest when it is translated into the role of one or more teachers. If we are to do more than pay lip-service to the evaluation of teacher performance, then we must clearly allocate responsibility for this when we define roles; and that allocation of responsibility must be in precise terms.

Often the main responsibility lies with a deputy, sometimes with a member of staff specifically appointed as staff tutor. The extent of the role of the head of faculty or senior member of his staff assigned by him to the task must be known. Plainly the probationer teacher must know the way in which his performance is being assessed and the expectation of him. At Kinslade School, in the 'dark ages' under its first headmaster, probation reports were prepared – if that is the word – with the minimum of consultation, and in an arbitrary fashion. Now, under Walter Truelove, a headmaster skilled in management techniques, the procedure is entirely different.

The newly qualified teacher learns through his colleagues that his first year of teaching is an extension of his professional training. Probationer teachers are encouraged to share their previous and their current experience with each other and with senior staff. Areas of difficulty must be identified and brought into the open. The criteria by which the probationer is to be judged are clearly set out, and are made known to him. The headings of the *pro forma* which the head of faculty completes are as follows:

TEACHING
Relationship with pupils, control, arousal of enthusiasm
Organization and planning of classwork
Organization and planning of preparation.

STAFF RELATIONS
Contribution to faculty team
Co-operation within faculty
Readiness to take advice
Attitude to colleagues in general.

PERSONAL
Thoroughness of pupil assessment, marking, correcting
Record of work
Punctuality
Particular strengths and weaknesses.

OTHER COMMENTS

The year head is also invited to comment on the probationer's ability as a tutor, as is the head of faculty or department of any area (drama, music, games) where the new teacher is making a voluntary contribution.

The head of faculty has discussed his comments with the probationer, often in the presence of a senior member of the faculty who is closer to the probationer and whose views have already contributed to what the head of faculty has written. The deputies add comments from their own observation and the file passes to the headmaster. He then writes a summary of these opinions and assessments, modified if need be by his own observation, in the form required by the Kemshire Education Department. The probationer sees and signs the office copy, and may of course question any statement which he thinks does him injustice. Should he so do (it happens rarely) the phraseology is looked at closely, the point at issue discussed with the senior member of staff who initiated it, and the statement modified if it does not correctly represent a true assessment. It may be that, after full consideration, the headmaster stands by his original formulation. Kemshire Education Department has no procedure whereby the probationer can show his dissent, except that he can discuss the matter with the county adviser who is required to see him at least once in his probation year.

Kinslade School's procedure is not county policy, but a number of Truelove's Kemshire colleagues (and those from less mythical regions of the British Isles who have met him on Kinslade School simulation courses!) are adopting this or similar procedures. The value in terms of human relations of this open policy of evaluation is considerable.

Constructing a role definition

The formulation of a role definition presents no problems. Figure 7 shows the main considerations.

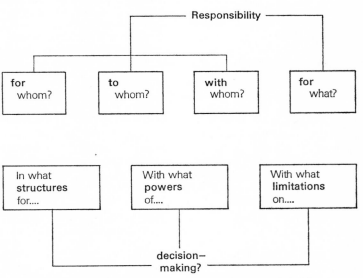

Figure 7. Considerations in constructing role definition

In Kinslade School there are four posts of responsibility in the humanities faculty, one at scale 4 and three at scale 3. In most schools these posts would be allocated on a basis of subject responsibility. The Kinslade humanities staff, however, have recognized that to stress subject specialization is to militate against a holistic approach in this subject area. The head of faculty has, therefore, three team leaders.

His own role is mainly co-ordinative. The upper school team leaders, a geographer and an historian, are each responsible for the academic progress of all pupils studying one or more humanities subjects in one upper school year, for a two-year cycle. The third post is designated 'Team leader: lower school humanities'. His role definition is as follows.

TEAM LEADER: LOWER SCHOOL HUMANITIES

1. To be responsible to head of humanities faculty for:
   (a) selection of themes
   (b) provision of resource material
   for integrated humanities syllabus in lower school.

2. To be responsible for selection and deployment of lower school humanities team, in liaison with appropiate deputy head and head of faculty, as far as general school staffing permits.

3. To lead his team in the detailed preparation of themes and evaluation of content. It is expected that each member of the team will contribute either a theme or a specialized part of a theme. The team leader's main responsibility is to ensure adequate coverage, provision of material for all ability ranges and reasonable balance of content.

4. To work with the head of faculty and the upper school team leaders (geography and history) as a member of the faculty curriculum development team.
   In particular:
   (a) to collaborate with the feeder schools and establish with them a 'bridging group' to (i) confer over aims and objectives, (ii) devise, where possible, a common-core content and (iii) interchange ideas and resources
   (b) to prepare third-year students for choice of upper school humanities option(s).

5. Within the financial limits allowed by the head of faculty, to select and order books, films and other resource materials.

6. To advise the librarian on library books suitable for lower school humanities students, for research and extensive reading.

7. To confer with team leaders in other faculties, as and when appointed, over the attainment levels in the lower school, and common problems.

Role definition in practice

Role definition has immediate practical uses, as well as contributing to the long-term well-being of the school. In staff selection it enables the potential applicant to judge the appropriateness of the role to him.[1] In other words, the applicant is in a position to interview the post before he applies for it. The time taken in preparing these details is amply compensated by the self-elimination of

[1] See Chapter 4, where this point is taken up in the context of the whole procedure for selecting the staff.

candidates who decide that, doubtless for a variety of reasons, this is not the post for them. In senior appointments, the ratio of those who write for details to those who submit applications has, in several schools which follow this practice, been two or three to one.

Very many secondary schools are involved in reorganization schemes. They are either waiting for them to come into effect, or are in the throes of them. Other schools are involved in growth situations. This may be a consequence of reorganization, if they are lucky enough not to have been subjected to wholesale changes, but have been enabled to grow organically. There may be a growth or a decline in the intake, the result of local government boundary changes, housing developments or slum clearance, changes in the age level of the local population, plans for overspill from the large conurbations. The development or disappearance of local industries, the influx or dissemination of immigrant population may radically affect the size or the nature of the school. To meet all these changes, new roles may need to be created, or the functions of existing roles may have to be modified. Since goals must always be decided before tasks are allocated it is evident that the acceptance in school management of the importance of role definition acts as a stimulus to the promotion of policy to meet changing conditions.

Even in relatively stable situations, role definition has an evaluative function. Each role definition should be regularly re-examined. Have the roles developed according to plan or has the organization of the school undergone a change, subtle rather than radical, that has had its effect on the pattern of the discharge of responsibilities? Has experience disclosed inequalities in the division of labour, not so glaring that it is obvious that the load carried by a particular member of staff is blatantly excessive but sufficient to suggest the need for some reallocation of responsibility? However stable the institution, a school is a social phenomenon and therefore, whether it wishes or no, reflects changes in society. Has the total purpose of the institution, then, become modified? If so, has this had any effect on the roles, creating new needs, or dispensing with old ones? Finally, in evaluating the functioning of a role, one is inevitably led to an evaluation of the functionary. Has the individual outgrown his role? Or, sadly, has the role outgrown him?

Role Conflict

I have written so far about role definition without explicitly men-
tioning role conflict. There are, however, very few situations
involving human relationships within a social institution which
do not give rise to role conflict. It is least likely in rigidly stratified
institutions, where there are overt prohibitions on going outside
one's terms of reference; in strictly authoritarian institutions,
where there is no delegation, only an allocation of tasks; and in
highly mechanistic institutions where the induced conformity
subordinates the individual to the symbol. Role conflict is most
likely in inchoate, permissive organizations lacking clearly defined
aims. It is also most likely in situations of rapid or extensive
change.

Elizabeth Richardson's depth study of Nailsea School[1] is a
unique example, at least in this country, of experiential research.
Because the school was undergoing radical change, from grammar
school to comprehensive school and in size, the book abounds in
examples of role conflict. Two quotations will suffice:

> Certainly many staff members, in redefining their own leadership
> roles, were compelled to re-examine, *at times in quite a painful
> way*, the basis of the authority they exercised in the school. [My
> italics]

and:

> In their different ways these three [middle-management staff] . . .
> were all struggling with the problem of defining their leadership
> roles in the school, not only in relation to pupils within a particular
> context of learning but also in relation to colleagues.

The existence of role conflict is unarguable. Any attempt to define
relationships is bound to open the door to the struggle for power
and the tensions of group dynamics. On the other hand, to avoid
the issue is also to open the door, but this door is the back door.
It is better to be aware of, and bring into the open, the areas most
likely to lead to conflict than to live in a fool's paradise, believing
that, if you do not think of it, it will go away.

I have set out to demonstrate throughout this chapter that role
definition has to do not only with tasks and objectives, but essentially with people; and there is a serious danger of creating a sense

[1] *The Teacher, the School and the Task of Management* (Heinemann Educational, 1973).

of euphoria if one does not think beyond those people who fill the roles that we have so carefully defined. Elizabeth Richardson hints at this in the phrase 'not only in relation to pupils', but it extends to the whole of the school's clientele: pupils, parents, employers, the community. The most elaborate complex of role definitions *within* the organization may be completely vitiated by the public expectation of one's role. To nobody does this apply more than to the headteacher.

Because the parents' experience is almost certainly confined to the school they attended as pupils, their expectation of the allocation of responsibilities within the school bears little relationship to the structure we may be seeking to create. 'I want to see the headmaster' says the parent, and the public image of the school is not enhanced by the reply, 'The headmaster does not deal with such matters.' Indeed, the headmaster may well have to deal with such matters, but if he is adept he will deal with them in such a way as to channel them painlessly to the person within whose role definition the problem falls. He may have to listen to the complaint or problem, and then offer to arrange an appointment with the member of staff concerned. He may have to deal with it himself, and act as a channel of communication to his teacher, transferring the continuation of the dialogue without the parent feeling he has been fobbed off. The headmaster will certainly have to demonstrate on public occasions where the responsibility lies. You cannot have devolution and the limelight. For example, though the headteacher and his deputies will undoubtedly attend a year meeting when parents and students discuss reports, option choices or careers with the year tutor and his pastoral staff, it must be clear that the invitation comes from the year tutor, that the arrangements are his and that his role and contribution are recognized and appreciated. Other staff, however senior, are in this situation acting in a supportive capacity. Role definitions are thus conveyed implicitly.

A growing familiarity with the school as an organization and the natural pleasure that parents of older children take in showing new parents the ropes – 'If I were you, I'd go and see Mrs C. She's the one who deals with . . .' – disseminate public knowledge of and public confidence in the roles assigned within the school. Nevertheless, we would be foolish to close our eyes to the complexities of our management structures. Even if we understand them clearly, it does not follow that those outside the structure will do so. After all, their organizational models are very different: for the housewife, the departmental store complaints department;

in the factory, the welfare officer or the shop steward; in the hospital, the almoner.

In considering the undoubted contribution to good management in schools of role definitions and clearly conceived allocation of responsibility we must not make the glib assumption that, once we have constructed the system, all will be well. It is salutary to remember that, though the roles may be functionally perfect, those who fill them are by nature functionally imperfect. Yet they have capacities for development, for the exercise of initiative, and the ability to summon up reserves of energy to meet sudden demands and crises that go beyond the limitations of any role we may define for them.

4 Selecting the staff

The power given to a headteacher over the selection of his staff varies considerably from one education authority to another. At one extreme, the governors of a secondary school may make all appointments, either as a body, or in the case of what seem to them to be 'unimportant posts' (those of the rank and file teachers, no less!) by delegation to a sub-committee or to the chairman. It is possible for the headteacher to have little or no say in the appointment; for his questions at interview to be limited or curtailed, or for his judgement on the suitability of a candidate to be overruled. In one authority the headmaster was required to set out in writing three questions, and only three, which the chairman would read to each candidate at the appropriate time during the interview. A now distinguished colleague, at that time a very inexperienced head, made the mistake of formulating his three questions in such a way that the first candidate was able to answer them very succinctly: 'Yes.' 'No.' 'Yes.' With a feeling not far removed from panic, the headteacher asked the chairman if he might ask a supplementary question. 'No, headmaster, you've had your three questions. We'll never be finished if we allow such latitude.'

At the other extreme, it is written into the articles of government of the secondary schools of one local education authority that the headteacher 'will appoint' assistant staff and the governing body 'will approve'. What happens if they disapprove is not stated, but some such safeguard is an obvious legal requirement, since the headteacher as an employee of the local education authority cannot in a contractual sense appoint another employee.

There are still authorities which differentiate between the powers of appointment vested in the headteachers of one type of school and another: secondary modern and grammar, in areas where reorganization has not taken place; even comprehensive and grammar, where such schools coexist. It is difficult to conceive of any justification for this differentiation. The local government reorganization of 1974 has ironed out some of these anomalies within and between education authorities, as new articles of government have been drafted, but they still exist.

These codified restraints on the power of the head teacher to appoint his staff are not the only limitations. He may be restricted by the practice of his local education authority in two respects: in the placing of advertisements for vacancies, and in the drawing up of the short-list of candidates for interview. Some authorities allow heads to submit their advertisements direct to the educational press, usually through an agency. Others require details of vacancies to be submitted to the education office, so that a consolidated advertisement can be placed. This may be more economical for the authority, but it will certainly extend the time between conception and delivery, and may, if the clerk concerned is instructed to follow a set formula, distort the true nature of the vacancy.

If applications have to be addressed to the local education authority, it is certain that the process of appointment to a vacancy will be further extended and likely that the authority's inspectorate will insist on being consulted over the drawing up of a list of those to be called to interview. Even when applications are made direct to the school, inspectors and advisers may expect to be consulted. A straw poll of a number of headteachers from the length and breadth of England and Wales showed that inspectors and advisers in physical education, music, drama, home economics, art and modern languages were the most likely to expect or insist upon consultation! Make of this what you will . . . The headteacher's freedom to act may be controlled by a further restraint, alternative or supplementary to those of the local education authority: the extent to which the governors of the school wish to be or are accustomed to being involved in the appointment. It may be that a precedent has been established, possibly when the school was smaller or staff changes less frequent, for the presence of a governor at every appointment. As will be seen below, there can be much merit in the 'neutral' chairman at interviews. Furthermore, with increasing representation of members of the local community on governing bodies, including parents and teachers, the presence of one governor at least may well make an effective contribution. For very senior appointments most headteachers expect the presence of a number of governors and at least one representative of the officers of the education authority.

Selection procedures

The variations in the constraints on the freedom of the head-teacher to appoint staff pale into insignificance compared with the wide range of practice between one head and another in his administration of the selection procedure. The two main factors by which he may be judged are the efficiency of his administration, and the extent to which he involves other staff in the process. Staffing vacancies, other than those which occur casually during the academic year, provide an opportunity for a reappraisal of staff requirements in detail. In a well managed school the effect of curriculum change on staff needs will be anticipated for a three-year period: for the coming year in precise detail, for the next two as a reasonable forecast. The growing or fading popularity of an option choice has its implications, unless the numbers admitted to an option are to be artificially controlled to coincide with the availability of staff. Each year, in February if he is fortunate, a headteacher is given his staffing quota for the next academic year. If the size of his school remains unchanged, he will be lucky to receive any increase in his quota; but a large majority of secondary schools today are in a state of flux, usually of expansion, and the utilization of additional resources should never be a matter of headmagisterial grace and favour, but of open debate. In brief, natural growth, reorganization, improved staffing ratios, changes in the points available for above scale posts, or a high percentage staff turnover must lead to a reappraisal of staffing needs.

Each school needs to keep under constant review the balances between teaching and non-teaching time of the staff as a whole. In terms of curriculum analysis the ratio between the number of periods which could be taught if *every* member of staff taught *every* period (heaven forbid!) and the number actually taught is known as the K factor.[1] This factor is likely to lie between 1·25 and 1·3 in most schools. There is no specific merit in the higher figure. More non-teaching time may be achieved at the expense of larger classes; or the distribution of non-teaching time may be unsatisfactory, imposing excessive burdens on certain areas of responsibility.

It is for this reason, if for no other, that the distribution of

---

[1] In the latest D.E.S. version on curriculum analysis this has become the C factor and is the reciprocal of the K factor. In other words 750 teaching periods out of 1000 possible teaching periods gives $C = ·75$. This is much easier to understand!

responsibility – outlined as a result of the role definition described
in the previous chapter – should be known to the staff as a whole,
and agreed by them. Similarly organizational and curricular
changes become the concern not of a select body but of the entire
staff, since their own teaching commitments may well be affected.
Obviously self-interest and unmoderated enthusiasms play a part
here, and it is the head's role to reconcile conflicting demands. He
will not do it, though he may appear to do so, by playing the
cards close to his chest. The secrets of the spring and summer
become open to all in the autumn timetable.

The specification of the vacancy

Self-evident though it may seem to be, it is important in staffing a
school to know what you want before you set out to get it. This
known, the specific nature of each post needs to be conveyed to
potential candidates. Plainly only the briefest and most essential
details can be conveyed in a press advertisement. An increasing
number of schools invite candidates to write, in the first instance,
for details of the school and post. The school prospectus must not
be a eulogistic self-advertisement. It ought succinctly to explain the
origins, organization and aims of the school, and give some general
picture of its social setting. The description of the post, drawn up
always in consultation with the senior member of staff with whom
the successful candidate will most closely work, needs to be no less
realistic. Dangled baits of 'possibility of A-level work at some time
in the future for a suitable candidate' or veiled hints of a later
upgrading of the post are despicable. The first implies that work
with more able and older pupils is a piece of candy for a teacher
who comes up to expectation. The latter makes it plain that the
school is run on nepotism, not open application for known posts
of responsibility.

The time taken in preparing these details is time well spent.
First, the information conveyed will obviate many of the candidate's questions. Secondly, there will be some, often an appreci-
able degree, of self-selection of candidates who see the post as too
or insufficiently demanding, or not matching their abilities, experience or interests.

Applications and References

Applications can be required on a printed form, or in a letter of
application accompanied by a curriculum vitae. Inevitably, when

applications have to be submitted through an education office, the printed form is used. Even when applications are submitted direct to schools, some heads still prefer the form. It has the advantages that no important detail is left out and that the tabulation of information for all candidates is identical, but it has many disadvantages. Some l.e.a. forms still ask questions like 'Do you play the piano?', an attribute which does not weigh very heavily in my selection of a mathematician or physical scientist. More importantly, the form is of necessity impersonal. Letters of application, however brief, will often contain the seeds of a useful discussion at interview. Some can be remarkably informative. Some can even be heart-rending! 'I have made a number of applications for posts of this kind,' an applicant to Kinslade School once wrote, 'and though my headmaster assures me I have his support, nobody ever calls me to interview. Please do, just this once!'

Very few authorities and fewer schools now ask for open testimonials. Except where a candidate has come from overseas and it might be difficult for the headteacher to get in touch speedily with a previous employer, they are valueless. Whoever submitted an adverse testimonial? They are more often personal than professional, and refer to the devoted assistance given by Miss A to the Brownies.

Two references are usually required, and many heads adopt the practice of stating that one, save in exceptional circumstances, must be from the present employer. This is not unreasonable (except, obviously, for first appointments, when candidates give their college or department of education as a reference). It has been known for candidates, in naming their present employer, to indicate that they do not expect their application to be supported. The reasons they give may be illuminating! The naming of a head of department or a deputy head and not the headteacher creates, if no cogent reason is given, a situation of some embarrassment. A headteacher would expect to write to a colleague of equal standing for a reference, and his opposite number would not expect to be bypassed. The naming of an l.e.a. inspector or adviser, and particularly the naming of a director of education creates another embarrassment, that of protocol. Most heads will ask their education offices to take up such a reference.

While teachers' unions have strict codes of professional conduct over the writing of confidential reports on colleagues – and rightly so – it is generally assumed that when an applicant asks his

headteacher or colleague if he may name him as a referee, he is
in so doing giving him *carte blanche* to write as he sees fit. One
headmaster sends out references which end, 'I have shown this
reference to Mr X, as is my practice . . .' Obviously he does not
regard himself as absolved from a professional obligation. I have
always taken the view that any reference which I give is intended
to help both parties, the applicant and the prospective employer.

	Out-standing	Good	Average	Barely satis-factory	Poor
Health					
Punctuality and attendance					
Personal/emotional stability					
Normal appearance and manner					
Ability to lead and inspire					
Soundness of judgement					
Initiative					
Dependability and co-operation					
Administrative efficiency (reports, records, organization, etc.)					
Personal relationships with staff					
Personal relationships with and understanding of pupils					
Lesson preparation and presentation					
Discipline and class control					
General willingness to work hard					

Figure 8. Profile reference

It is not for me to be an advocate for the former or the arbiter for
the latter, but to present a fair picture of the applicant's attributes
and shortcomings. A headteacher can obviously be of more use
to his colleague and to the member of his staff if he knows the

details of the school and the post. Here the information prepared for the candidate obviously has a further use, and is sent out automatically with the request for a reference. The covering letter can usually be a standard one, but if cyclostyled it should leave room for any specific question arising from the application to be written or typed in. A number of headteachers have adopted five-point scale[1] profiles for the referee to complete. It is likely that their precedent for this form of evaluation is the profile reference used by the Services and some employers.

The profile is obviously designed to make objective the assessment by the referee of a candidate. It has the advantage that all the points for which the prospective employer would like a comment are included in the reference. Its main disadvantage is that many of the criteria are themselves highly subjective. What, for example, is the compiler's criterion of normalcy in the heading 'Normal appearance and manner'? And how can he evaluate *my* assessment if he does not know *my* criterion? A subsidiary disadvantage is that the referee is being forced into standardized assessments without the possibility of qualification. I may wish to say that 'in general the candidate's personal relationships with staff are extremely good, but that he has from time to time overreacted against what appears to him to be unwarranted criticism from senior members of staff, though he may later, after much discussion, have accepted its justification.' I am forced, however, into one of five dehydrated statements, none of which suits my purpose. A five-point scale denies the vagaries and inconsistencies of human nature. Scientific objectivity should be reserved for that which can be scientifically assessed. Nevertheless one can appreciate the reasons why some headteachers may be seeking an alternative to the usual letter of reference. Here is a reference for a candidate for a drama post at Kinslade School which does little credit to the writer:

[1] The five-point scale was devised by an American called Likert in the 1930s. It is really an *attitude* test, and takes the form of a series of statements. For example: 'In the interest of permanent peace, we should be willing to put to arbitration absolutely all differences with other nations which we cannot settle by diplomacy.' Five points are then allocated to the answer 'strongly approve', four to 'approve', down to one to 'strongly disapprove'. The Likert scale has been much criticized by modern social psychologists. It is too narrow; the midpoint ('undecided') has no real meaning, and is as likely to be an escape from commitment as a genuine statement of opinion; there is no evaluation of the relative importance of items; and consequently the score has no absolute meaning.

Dear Headmaster,

This is a school with a long tradition of sound
academic achievement, and it is only in the past
four years that it has had a drama teacher.
Mr Carr was appointed by my predecessor, at a
time when the head of English, as a result of the
pressure of his A-level commitments, no longer
felt able to produce the annual school play. Mr
Carr possesses a great deal of self-confidence
and will undoubtedly interview well. He has shown
a certain amount of enterprise, and we have had
several plays put on since he came, not all of
which I have been able to see because of pressure
of other commitments. Drama is also on the timetable for the younger pupils.

Mr Carr has been very ready to take parties on
theatre visits, mostly, however, to matinées in
school time. As an English teacher he has prepared
one set of candidates for O level, and the results
were not outstandingly good, in spite of the fact
that our weaker pupils are now entered for the
C.S.E. However, I believe he may have benefited
from the experience.

Mr Carr is quite popular amongst pupils and colleagues and would probably work well as a member
of a team. I do not know why he wants to move to
your area. I can only imagine that he is attracted
by the financial advantages of the scale post that
a school as large as yours is able to offer.

Yours faithfully,

J. M. Brown

Headmaster

It is a truism that a reference tells you as much about the referee
as about the candidate.

The main uses of references are twofold. They are one element,
but only one, in the production of the short-list of candidates for
interview. There are times when an adverse reference merely
indicates that a candidate and his headteacher are incompatible.
There are also times, regrettably, when a glowing reference dis-
guises the fact that a headteacher is longing to see the back of a
member of staff. Far more importantly, the reference indicates
to the headteacher key areas to be explored when the candidate

is invited to interview. And here there is a dilemma of professional ethics. An increasing number of headteachers are involving their deputies and other senior staff in short-listing and in the interviewing process. The reference is, however, a confidential document, and not to be circulated with a candidate's application. Indeed, there are times when details on the application itself need to be treated as confidential. The candidate may, in explaining his reasons for wishing to make a move from his present post, reveal facts or opinions which he would not wish colleagues on the staff of his new school, were he appointed, to be aware of. All in all, it is best for the curriculum vitae, or an abstract of it, to be circulated to members of staff involved in the interview, and any material which could conceivably be regarded as confidential to remain with the headteacher.

There are strong arguments for and against the use of the telephone in obtaining or giving a reference. It saves time. It enables the headteacher to engage in a dialogue with the referee, probing in greater depth those areas of assessment which seem to him of greater importance. He is far more likely to be able to judge whether he and the referee have similar sets of values. Against this is the obvious accusation of 'the old boy network', the difficulty of presenting a balanced judgement as referee if you are having to switch from consideration of some domestic issue, and the plain fact that the recipient's notes of the conversation may, a week later, do less than justice to the referee's views.

The interview

It is common courtesy to candidates aᵢ their present headteachers to give them reasonable notice of the interview, and to indicate road and rail routes to the town or city, the route to the school and the length of time which should be allowed. For major appointments it is often possible to state the date of interview on the details of the post, and consequently the date by which short-listed candidates can expect to have heard. Candidates ought to be given a clear indication of how the time at the school will be spent; they should be told the authority's scale of travel and subsistence allowances and offered help with arrangements for overnight accommodation if this is necessary. The invitation to interview should also list any information or evidence of qualification required at the interview or after selection. In return for these courtesies, which a remarkable number of teachers tell me they rarely receive, the headteacher has a right to expect a return-of-post acceptance or refusal of the invitation by the candidate. If the candidate has another interview before this one, he should say so. Last-minute withdrawals are a great inconvenience to the interviewing school. The consequent last-minute invitation to interview of another candidate is a certain indication to him that he is only a reserve!

The formal interview is without doubt the least important part of the proceedings when the candidates come to the school. After nearly twenty years of interviewing I still do not have the expertise to make judgements that will affect the future of a school solely on the basis of twenty minutes' question and answer. For the sake of both the candidate and the school it is essential that the 'interview' includes the opportunity to meet and talk with colleagues and pupils, to see teaching situations, facilities and resources and to ask questions freely of whomsoever he wishes. At the same time the candidate must accept that he is being assessed in these discussions, even by his reactions to what he observes as he goes round the school. Some schools favour a series of interviews with different members of staff, each with clearly defined terms of reference. Others prefer a less structured approach in which the onus is mainly on the candidate to ask what he wants to know.

A candidate must have the opportunity to withdraw before the interview if he wishes. Once many local education authorities ruled that a candidate who did so forfeited his expenses. If any still do so today, it is time they abandoned this practice, demeaning to both the candidate and the interviewer. Any candidate forced into this position should 'throw' the interview in the most outrageous manner possible, so that he is rejected!

If a candidate may withdraw, should a headteacher not have the same right to curtail the proceedings for an obviously unsuitable candidate *before* the formal interview? I will never appoint to a faculty, for example, an applicant with whom the head of faculty could not work amicably. If this has become abundantly clear to all except the candidate, am I not wasting valuable time in proceeding further? However, if candidates have not already been told that they may not be called upon for the final stage of selection, it is only courteous to continue.

The length of the formal interview should not exceed twenty minutes: with four candidates the interviewing session will last at least two hours, and that is stretching the panel's concentration to its limits. What is important is that the twenty minutes is used to the best advantage. Preparation for the interview and the skilled use of interviewing techniques are both essential. It is general practice for a panel of four or five to appoint to senior posts, and of two or three to first appointments and junior posts. The presence of a member of the governing body may be insisted upon. In any case it may well be useful if the chair is taken by someone other than the headteacher, since he is then more free to observe a candidate's reactions (and sometimes evasions!) if he has not this responsibility. Whatever the size of the panel it is imperative that the headteacher plans in advance, even with those staff who will not be on the interviewing panel, the areas of questioning and the conduct of the interview.

Candidates must have a waiting area, conveniently near the place of interview, but if possible away from the inquisitorial gaze of the curious. If it can be arranged, a senior member of staff, not otherwise involved in the interviewing, should be in attendance to answer individual questions, not least those about the price and availability of accommodation. Candidates should be told the membership of the panel, the probable timings and the batting order. Many a Taylor or a Williams has complained bitterly that he is always last in, and has been staggered by the suggestion that candidates should draw lots for the order of their going. If there is an internal candidate for a post of seniority, he should join the candidates at this stage, and they should have been told of his candidature from the outset. He should not appear like a rabbit out of a hat. If he proves to be the successful candidate, the others must at least have the chance of being convinced from their own observation that he was the best man.

The interviewers must have a single sheet précis of the candidate's details, with room for notes; or, alternatively, a photocopy of the candidate's curriculum vitae. Brief discussion of the areas of questioning before the candidate enters is valuable. References are not appropriate at this stage, but extracts from the letter of application may be useful pointers to relevant questions. The physical layout of the room for the interview is not unimportant. The panel should not be ranged in a long line so that the candidate suffers from Wimbledon neck. Some favour an informal grouping of seats, others like tables for their documents. Distractions must be prevented at all costs. Internal telephone systems are a particular hazard.

An interview will only begin satisfactorily when rapport is established. It is the chairman's role to see that the candidate is mentally at ease. He does this best with a few 'comfortable' questions, and the candidate ought to appreciate that the answers to

these are known already to the panel, and maintain a commendable brevity. The technique of questioning has received scant
attention in education – strange in a profession which asks so many
questions! It is wrong, moreover, to assume that the techniques
used by a teacher to elicit response from his pupils are identical
with the techniques of the interviewer.

What does the interviewer seek to discover? Explicitly, the
educational aims of the candidate; the extent to which he has
been able to realize these aims – and even a candidate for first
appointment has had, it must be appreciated, some opportunity
to do so, whatever the constraints; his knowledge of his subject
and of the skills required to redeploy his knowledge for students
of a variety of ages, levels of attainment and degrees of interest;
and, not least, his powers of self-analysis and likely response to
criticism and advice. Implicitly, what kind of person he is.

This is, to say the least, a tall order for twenty minutes. It is not
made easier by the fact that most interviewers say too much and
listen too little. In a number of years of running vacation courses
for headteachers and senior staff I have, in the interview simulation exercise, kept a surreptitious stop-watch on the actual time a
candidate has been enabled to talk. In the best interviews this may
reach 70 per cent of the interview time. In many it is no more
than 40 per cent or 50 per cent. In other words, for at least half
the time the interviewers have been doing the talking! Plainly,
little is learnt about the candidate when he is the listener, except
perhaps his composure and his attentiveness. The mere answering
of questions is, however, of little merit unless the questions are well
formulated. Closed questions, those that demand the answer 'yes'
or 'no', are rarely productive unless the candidate takes the
initiative to open them. 'Did you enjoy your tour of the school
this morning?' is pointless. 'What have you seen in the school that
you particularly liked, or of which you are particularly critical?'
is a much more profitable question. It gives the candidate considerable initiative, it applies a reasonable degree of stress on the
candidate (and an interview without stress will reveal little of a
candidate's ability to cope with the stresses of the profession) and
it gives the opportunity for follow-up questions which may give
greater depth to the sequence.

Leading questions are also to be avoided. 'Can you keep order?'
rates zero. 'How do you deal with difficult control situations?' will
produce a more meaningful response. Some interviewers like to
describe a situation and ask for the candidate's reaction. 'A boy
in your class pulls a chair away from a girl just as she is about to

sit down. What do you do?' Those who ask questions of this type must expect an apparently evasive response from some candidates. 'It all depends on who the boy is, who the girl is, the reaction of the rest of the class and the circumstances that led to the incident' is as reasonable a reply as a step-by-step (I trust not a blow-by-blow) account of what he would do.

Open-ended questions have their dangers, nevertheless. They may lead to loss of control of the interview. To quote G. C. White's excellent pamphlet[1] for the Central Youth Employment Executive: 'In practice, it is probably best to start off a topic with open-ended questions, using closed questions as supplementaries to fill in details that are important.'

Multiple questions are as maddening for the candidate as for other members of the interviewing panel. 'At your present school do you enjoy your work with older pupils more than with younger pupils? Or has the raising of the school leaving age made a difference? By the way, they do start at twelve, not eleven, don't they? Is this a good idea?' Such questions are probably only a test of a candidate's patience and diplomacy. The best answer may well be 'Yes', leaving the questioner to sort out the question to which this is the reply. Far too many interviewers worry their questions to death. They may do this in two ways. First, they ask a question, and then – particularly if the candidate pauses for a moment's thought – re-word it. The phrase 'I mean' is a sure indicator of this annoying habit. Secondly, interviewers insist on pursuing a topic long after they have learnt enough of the candidate's viewpoint to make a reasonable assessment of his attitude. It is no part of an interview to convince a candidate that he is wrong and you are right. The only justification for argument is to place a candidate under pressure.

I have used the words 'stress' and 'pressure', and it may be felt by many victims that the interviewing procedure in itself imposes quite enough strain. Nevertheless, particularly in appointing staff who will have to carry the burdens of others from time to time, it is essential to get below the surface. Most of us enter an interview

[1] *Careers Bulletin Supplement: Research* (September 1970, No. 2), G. C. White, *Interviewing Techniques*. Written primarily for careers guidance officers, this booklet gives more sound commonsense advice in nine pages than most of the scholarly literature on interviewing and selection that fill the shelves of university and polytechnic management departments. However, he refers to two publications which deserve further study by those particularly interested: A. R. Rodger, *Seven Point Plan* (National Institute of Industrial Psychology, 1970); and M. Argyle, *The Psychology of Interpersonal Behaviour* (Penguin, 1967).

behind some kind of *persona* or mask, demonstrating what we would like to be thought to be, and not what we are. It will take more than an interview to evaluate the real man: his reality will only become apparent in the interplay of personalities faced with human situations. Imperfect instrument though the interview may be, it must make some attempt to penetrate the outer shell.

There are those who cannot bear silences in an interview. Often silences can be more meaningful than words. A good questioner will distinguish between the pause for consideration and the end of a reply. The candidate, too, will value a respite before a complete change of topic. The attitude of those on the panel who are not currently engaged in the dialogue is important. Shuffles, doodles or asides are not conducive to good candidate response. On the other hand, evidence of general interest and non-oral cues, nods, smiles and so on, extend the candidate's motivation and appreciativeness. White quotes an American experiment in which 'interviews were divided into three 15-minute periods. The interviewer spoke for 5 seconds at a time throughout but, during the middle period only, nodded encouragingly every time the applicant spoke'. The results shown in Figure 9 indicate the effect on response in terms of the length of time the applicant spoke.

	Interviewer spoke	Applicant spoke
1st period	5·1 secs	36·9 secs
2nd period (nods)	5·1 secs	54·7 secs
3rd period	5·1 secs	35·4 secs

Figure 9. The effect of encouragement in interviewing

To what extent can the formality of an interview be broken down, so that a series of duologues controlled by the chairman becomes a continuous, loosely structured dialogue in which the interviewing panel seeks to draw the candidate into group discussion? This presupposes a considerable degree of mutual understanding on the part of the panel, but is not impossible. It works best in small-group situations, when two or three at most are interviewing, and there is no need for a chairman. Most young candidates appreciate this format, in my experience, finding it less exacting than the interview situation they had anticipated. Some older candidates are disturbed, because it runs counter to their experience and expectation.

Whatever the form of the interview it should be drawn to a close with an invitation from the chairman or headteacher to the candidate to ask any questions he wishes. It should be made clear that there is no merit in asking questions for the sake of doing so. More than once my heart has sunk to my boots as a candidate takes from an inside pocket a sheet of paper saying, 'I just jotted these down in the train as I came.' If a candidate's questions have not been answered outside the interview room, then there must be something wrong with my preparation, or the candidate's trust in my colleagues' ability to answer him truthfully. On occasions, however, there are relevant questions. Sometimes they have arisen from the interview itself, or from what the candidate has seen but felt it inappropriate to ask before the interview. On one occasion the headmaster of Kinslade School was asked, 'What made *you* come here?' and 'How long do you intend to stay?' Both questions he regarded as reasonable, and answered to the best of his ability.

The final question is of the utmost importance. It is 'If you were offered the post, would you accept it?' If a candidate wishes to have a quiet think outside the interview room, he should be entitled to it. It is to be hoped that he is not the last candidate, and that his thinking is not prolonged. What of the candidate who is not prepared to give an acceptance that day? He should be told the implications, whatever they may be in this particular situation, of his indecision. Given two candidates of equal merit, he cannot expect the post to be kept open for him at the expense of the other. In certain circumstances, his request may be reasonable, even praiseworthy. Whatever the reply to the question, the panel needs to know before they deliberate.

At the end of the interviews, the panel should immediately agree on unanimous exclusions. It is a waste of time to analyse the reasons. The panel's task is to appoint, not pat itself on the back for its perception. Next it will wish to re-examine the written evidence submitted by the final candidates, hear the references, and discuss analytically and objectively. At this stage it is my practice to invite in the senior members of staff who have had contact with the candidates during the day. Observations like 'Never once did he speak to a pupil all the time we toured the school' would be, for me, fairly conclusive evidence that this is not the man for the school. At other times my colleagues' questions to the panel about a candidate's response in the interview situation may be sufficient to trigger off a decision. The governors of most schools will, it is to be hoped, take the view that, since the head-teacher and his staff have to work with the successful candidate, the final decision must be made by them. I am strongly opposed to situations in which the choice is made by vote. This has always seemed to me too facile an alternative to the application of logic and judgement. The successful candidate needs to know that he has the unqualified support of the panel, however difficult the process of choice may have been. It is essential to bear in mind that the aim of the selection procedure is to choose, not the best candidate, but the best candidate for the job. In doing so, con-sideration of a candidate's potentiality for development is often more important than a forecast of his immediate performance.

BEFORE THE INTERVIEW

| DECIDE | Precise nature of vacancy

| DRAFT | Advertisement, details of post

| DEAL WITH | Applications, enquiries, invitations

THE INTERVIEW

| PLAN |　　　Conduct of interview
　　　　　　Panel of interviewers
　　　　　　Disposition of time
　　　　　　Area of questioning

| PREPARE |　　Reception of candidates
　　　　　　Précis of particulars
　　　　　　Conditions for interview

| PERFORM |　　Establish rapport
　　　　　　Ask and listen
　　　　　　Invite questions
　　　　　　Evaluate

| SELECT |

AFTER THE INTERVIEW

The successful candidate:　　　The unsuccessful candidates:

| INTRODUCE TO |　other staff　| THANK | those interviewed

| INFORM |　other staff　| INFORM | other applicants

| PROCESS APPLICATION |

Figure 10. Summary of staff selection process

There remain only the courtesies and administrative details: the introduction of the successful candidate to his colleagues (but not to too many, poor devil!); thanks to the unsuccessful candidates and to the interviewers; such forms as are required by the education office.

Is there any alternative to a process which, in a large school, may occupy a headteacher for at least twenty working days out of the two hundred to which he is theoretically committed? The most obvious is that there should be devolution of responsibility for appointing teaching staff, as there is in most schools for the appointment of ancillary staff. This would in all probability be limited to appointments at Scale 1, but there are few logical objections to such appointments being decided by the head of faculty and a deputy head. The former will judge the candidate's pedagogic suitability, and the latter will act as a monitor of the candidate's potential in identifying with the staff as a whole and the educational and social aims of the school. Since the headteacher must on no account appear to be a remote figure, or the situation one of abdication rather than devolution, he must meet the candidates at some stage of the selection; but if he is not to be directly involved in the selection procedure, there is no reason why he should not meet them collectively, informally – perhaps over a cup of coffee when they arrive – and with the object of answering rather than asking questions. When at the end of the day the suitable candidate has been selected, the headteacher must of course, since the responsibility for offering an appointment must ultimately be and be seen to be his, formally appoint. Where his colleagues may be undecided between the merits of two applicants, the headteacher may be called upon to arbitrate. In such a case he needs to be well briefed on the merits and shortcomings that his colleagues have discovered, so that he can probe more deeply.

This suggestion will alarm those who see the headteacher as the 'captain of his ship' responsible for the performance of every deckhand and cabin-boy. If authority is what is required for the proper functioning of a school, then his authority will undoubtedly appear to be eroded. If, on the other hand, we are looking for collective responsibility, then this procedure will not only contribute to that, it will have the added merit of giving valuable experience to those who may one day, as headteachers themselves, have the overall responsibility of staff selection. Will it lead to the packing of a faculty with little images of the head of the faculty? There is this danger, and if there is an entrenched conflict of educational objectives between factions on the staff, then this could lead to partisan recruitment. A headteacher who has not brought into the open and sought to reconcile this conflict has, however, failed already to achieve collective responsibility, and it would be either premature or plainly foolish for him to abdicate from the role to which he was appointed. A good school tolerates a wide spectrum of educational opinion. Moreover, in a school where there is genuine participation in decision-making, the thorn in the flesh may even become the leaven in the lump.

Indeed, there exists in every school, whatever its style of management, the danger that in the selection of staff conformity – whether to radical or conservative educational aims – will be looked for, rather than compatibility. The key to the successful operation of all human institutions lies in personal relationships. These are founded on trust, tolerance, the willingness to learn from others and to share knowledge and experience with others. In his book *My Secret Diary*, Giovanni Guareschi, the author of the famous and wonderfully compassionate Don Camillo books, writes: 'All the living are bound by imperceptible radiations, like threads, together.' It is well worth remembering that each new staff appointment adds a thread. For both the candidate and the school the selection procedure has an importance, both immediate and long-term, which cannot be overstated.

5 Consultation procedures

We have seen in Chapter 2 the growth of complex organizational structures both for the furtherance of pastoral care and for the development of the curriculum. What we now need is a way in which these two structures can be brought into relationship with each other, harmoniously to work towards the common goal, the good of the student. At first sight, the solution is simple enough.

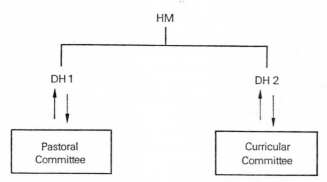

Figure 11. Pastoral and curricular structure – stage 1

As Figure 11 shows, the school stands on two legs, one labelled 'pastoral' and the other 'curricular' and each has its leader, a deputy in close contact with the headteacher. There will be a two-way flow in the decision-making procedure: from the committees to the head, and from the head to the committees. Immediately the question arises: who serves on these committees? Surely there is no doubt, you will say – the holders of the senior pastoral roles (year tutors or housemasters/mistresses) constitute the first committee, and the holders of senior curricular roles (heads of faculty) the second. Perhaps you are worried that these committees are perpetuating a hierarchical structure? Then let us build in a further tier of consultation, to ensure that there is a further two-way flow, to the tutors or the members of each faculty. Figure 12

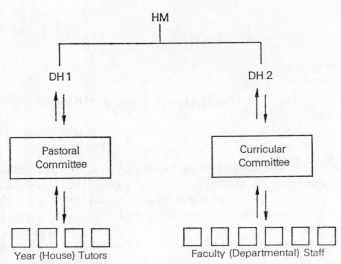

Figure 12. Pastoral and curricular structure – stage 2

shows a structure in which every member of staff has a place.
Our awkward questioner is still with us. What is the remit of each
committee? Self-evident, one would have thought, in their titles.
But is it as simple as this? Are there not decisions on the curriculum which concern pastoral staff, and on pastoral affairs which
concern curricular staff?

Let us take, for example, the decision to introduce a new option,
economics, into the curriculum, or to teach housecraft to both
boys and girls. In each case the pastoral staff are much involved.
They will have to explain these decisions to parents and pupils,
and in the first case will undoubtedly be involved in guidance. A
decision by the pastoral committee that there should be a weekly
house period similarly cannot be taken in isolation. The time must
come from somewhere, and that 'where' is undoubtedly very much
the concern of the curricular committee.

If these issues are to be debated in the present structure, then
they will have to travel down both legs. Yet the staff at the bottom
of each leg are the same people! This will not prevent them from
coming to different decisions according to the roles they are playing and the influences upon them of their senior staff and their
colleagues in each situation. Decisions, therefore, will only be
reached by a long drawn out process; and, because the expectations of certain groups of staff will not be met, there will be frustration and friction. We need therefore to look for a less cumbrous
machinery; and we need to look particularly at two levels, the

'shop floor' and the 'top management'. We must differentiate between those issues which can be regarded as falling clearly within the province of staff as tutors, or staff as subject teachers, and those in which a reconciliation of interests is needed. The latter requires the involvement of the staff as a whole. At the same time there needs to be co-ordination in the top management. What appears to be clear differentiation of function between Deputy 1^1 and Deputy 2 is in practice a departmentalism which will at best lead to lack of understanding and at worst to conflict. They should be brought together with the headteacher, and perhaps with other key members of staff, as the *staff management group* (Figure 13).

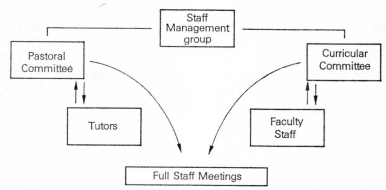

Figure 13. A possible decision-making structure based on a staff management group

The role of the staff management group

It is essential that we know what we mean by a staff management group. The H.M.A. pamphlet *The Government of Schools* states: 'the headmaster may find it helpful to meet regularly with a "cabinet" of very senior colleagues . . .' This, it may ingenuously be argued, is our staff management group. A closer examination of the wording, particularly in the context of the pamphlet as a whole, reveals that the autocracy, whether benevolent or otherwise, implicit in the self-assigned role of many headmasters is

1 I use the word 'deputy' instead of 'senior master/mistress' (which either post might well be) both for convenience and because, since 1971, the senior master/mistress has been paid the same salary as the deputy. It is high time the Burnham Committee woke up to the fact, and simply called the two – or, in larger schools, three – holders of posts next in seniority to the headteacher *deputies*.

being shored up by other, like-minded professional colleagues. The use of the word 'cabinet' cannot be casual. It implies for the headmaster the status of prime minister, who may turn to his colleagues for advice, but who is not bound to heed it. They are, it hardly needs to be said, of the same party, and though they may collectively offer a range of solutions to a problem, that range has clear limitations. Indeed the headmaster has advantages over the prime minister. He has security of tenure which the latter may well envy. The prime minister must seek from time to time, through the ballot box, public approval of his policies. Having placed the members of his cabinet in certain positions of responsibility which call for particular expertise and having allowed them to demonstrate that expertise to the country, both in parliament and out, it is with difficulty that he ignores their advice. If he loses the confidence of his colleagues in the cabinet, or indeed in the Commons, he may be overturned by a 'palace revolution'. It is scarcely surprising that an association of headmasters should be concerned with what a headmaster may find helpful in maintaining his authority on well-established lines. It should come as no greater surprise, then, for the reader to learn that the sentence quoted concludes as follows: '. . . of very senior colleagues, members by virtue of their offices *or his invitation*' [My italics]. One is forced to the cynical conclusion that if, by some grave miscalculation, the headmaster has not appointed to the appropriate offices (presumably the deputyships) those who will be 'helpful', he enlarges the cabinet until he is sure that he holds the reins. The pyramid of power has not changed shape. The apex has merely changed from a point to a triangle. One is left wondering why the H.M.A. should make even this change. Earlier in the pamphlet it produces the argument: 'Because a headmaster's standing is dependent upon the well-being of his school . . . he is in a position to make disinterested decisions on educational grounds.' Why then, if we complete the logic of the argument, seek the collaboration of those whose standing is not dependent upon the well-being of his (the headmaster's) school? How will he 'find it helpful to meet' those who, lacking this dependency, may make *biased* decisions on *non-educational* grounds?

The staff management group is not, therefore, a cabinet. Though it may not be appointed as an alter ego of the headteacher, it may still be an instrument of his authority. The crucial question is this: for whose benefit does it manage? In industry, such a body will manage for gain. Incidentally, it will also manage for the good of the workers, since on them (negatively, the absence of strikes;

positively, quality control) depends to a great extent the margin of profit. In education, there can be no such simple objective. The staff management group manages for the good of the school. The school is not 'his' (the headteacher's) nor 'theirs' (the staff's). Neither is it the pupils' nor their parents'. It is, whatever the complexity of the state machinery by which it is run, ultimately the community's.

In her excellent article in *Secondary Education*[1] Valerie Perry identifies six patterns of management, which show various ways in which the principles of consultative management may be put into effect. She obviously subscribes most strongly to Pattern VI and I quote it in full.

(i) Monthly full staff meeting chaired by headteacher. Adoption or rejection of committee reports, discussion and decision on policy changes.

(ii) Monthly pastoral committee. Year tutors, house tutors, plus one representative from each of the committes *(iii)*, *(iv)*, *(v)*. (Well-being of pupils, support services, careers.)

(iii) Monthly curriculum committee. Heads of department plus one representative from each of the committees *(ii)*, *(iv)*, *(v)*. (Curriculum, timetabling, new appointments (subject), probationers, allocation of capitation allowances.)

(iv) Monthly finance committee. Elected by staff. One representative from each of the committees *(ii)*, *(iii)*, *(v)*. (All school funds other than capitation allowances.)

(v) Monthly staff-room committee. Elected by staff. One representative from each of the professional associations. (Well-being of staff, working conditions.)

(vi) *Ad hoc* committees, working parties – as and when required. Appointed by and answerable to the staff meeting.

Implicit in this structure are the following features:

(i) All members of staff would be eligible to serve on at least one of the committees.

(ii) The majority of staff would be involved in not more than two meetings a month; some would be involved in three or four meetings a month.

(iii) Cross-representation would contribute to the smooth running of the committees.

(iv) All routine matters (once certain principles had been established) would then be implemented immediately following committee meetings and would then be ratified at the next staff meeting.

[1] Valerie Perry, 'Consultation in large secondary schools', *Secondary Education*, Vol. 4, No. 3 (June 1974).

(v) Changes of policy would require time for full discussion and consideration before any decision could be made (such as streaming/mixed-ability groups, range of subjects to be offered).

(vi) The terms of reference of each committee would not preclude discussion on a policy change. For example, changes in the pattern of the school day, where such a subject could obviously affect the pupil (pastoral committee), timetabling of subjects (curriculum committee), the working conditions of teachers (staff-room committee). Proposals emanating from any one of these committees would be submitted to the staff meeting.

(vii) The staff meeting would make the final decision which would become the staff's considered advice to the headteacher.

The great merit of this structure is that it makes the 'body politic' the staff as a whole, responsible for the formulation of policy, whatever devolution of that responsibility it may, in the interest of

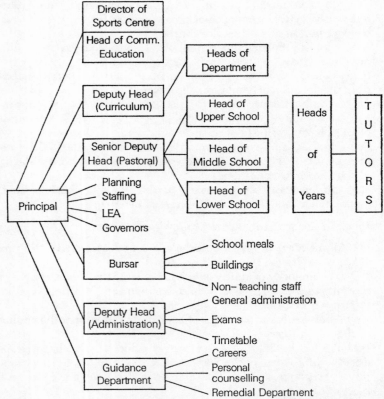

Figure 14. Structure of Portslade School and Community College, East Sussex

efficiency, decide upon. Its one weakness lies in the absence of a group charged with the task of seeing that policy, once formulated, is put into practice. It might be argued that this is the function of the headteacher and his deputies. If so, their place in the management structure, and the extent of their role, requires definition.

Portslade School and Community College is a large comprehensive school to the west of Brighton in East Sussex. Its size, its multiple role in that it is both school and community college, and the fact that it is on two sites have all played a part in the establishment of the complex structure shown in Figure 14.

Bob Glover, the Principal, has established a two-tier management structure, which is best explained by quoting from his staff handbook:

> *The Senior Management Team* meets weekly. It is composed of the principal, the deputy heads, the heads of lower, middle and upper school, and the head of community education. Its role is to discuss major matters of policy and to make recommendations to the School Management Committee. Minutes of meetings of this body will be published and may be the subject of discussion and decision by the School Management Committee.
>
> *The School Management Committee* is the main policy-making body of the establishment. Its decisions are binding upon the staff and students and are subject only to the reserve power of veto by the principal. It is also the executive committee of the establishment and all important matters for decision should come before this committee either as an agenda item or in the form of a minute of one of the School Management Committee's sub-committees.
>
> The School Management Committee consists of two categories of members: 'mandatory' and 'elective'. Mandatory members are the principal, deputy heads, heads of lower, middle and upper school, heads of department, head of community education, director of sports centre, heads of year and the school counsellor. 'Elective' members are any other members of staff who wish to attend. All members of staff have equal voting rights.
>
> Three students, elected by the School Council, attend School Management Committee meetings to present School Council minutes. They may attend for other items on the agenda at the discretion of the staff members of the committee.
>
> The principal is the chairman of the School Management Committee.

This structure has in it two important features which distinguish it radically from any structure that has been described so far:

> The Senior Management Team is *not* the policy-making body of the school.

The School Management Committee, which *is* the policy-making body is open to all members of staff who have rights equal to those exercised by members who are there by virtue of their status.

The role of the executive team

Because I have previously used the phrase *staff management group* to indicate a body which, while very different from the autocracy or oligarchy implicit in mechanistic establishments, nevertheless sees its place in the chain of command as a dominant one, I intend to use *executive team* to refer to a staff group which regards itself as charged with the task of policy implementation.

The executive team is not, fundamentally, a decision-making body, though to implement policy it will have to make decisions. Its role is:

1. to identify the areas in which decisions have to be made;
2. to establish an order of priority for decision-making;
3. to prepare or to invite from others the preparation of evidence – whether factual or in the form of a statement of a number of possible courses of action and their likely consequences – upon which a decision may be reached;
4. to implement that decision;
5. to evaluate the effectiveness of the implementation of a decision.

It is easy to define such a role. It is less easy, without a specific example, to envisage how such a role can be discharged.

At Kinslade School, at the end of the first term after the raising of the school leaving age, it became obvious that curricular preparation for the majority of the enforced stayers had been inadequate. It also became evident that, however urgent or important other areas of decision-making might be, for the staff this area was crucial. Indeed in many ways all other areas of decision-making might be said to depend upon changes to be made here.

The executive team met and identified the areas in which changes might be possible. Immediately it gave notice to the staff as a whole that it regarded this as a topic of such importance that it would be the main item of business for the first staff meeting of the next term. Staff were invited to give consideration to it, and formulate specific proposals, individually or through their faculty meetings. Early next term the executive team met two senior members of staff whose responsibilities lay largely with these pupils. One in particular had drafted a paper, the final version of which is reproduced in some detail, since the problems it poses will not have disappeared from our schools by the time this book is published, or for many years to come. (I write 'the final version' because discussion with the executive team led to the rephrasing of part of the original paper; but had the member of staff regarded the rephrasing as an attempt to water down his paper it would have been presented to staff as *he* wished, leaving the executive team free to dissent if it so wished.)

Observation on RoSLA

1. No school was entirely prepared for the problems peculiar to the first compulsory fifth year and we must now admit that this school was less prepared that we would have liked.

2. Few courses had been devised or adapted to the needs of these students.

3. Even where it was accepted that these students were not pursuing a course leading to examinations, the bulk of the work available to them was still too close to normal 'examination' work.

4. In mixed-ability groups some non-examination students were having, by Christmas, less than their share of staff time and school resources.

5. Of those students entered for a small number of examinations many find that a lot of their time is 'wasted' and that their frustrations are increasing.

6. Students who have decided to leave at Easter see no point in pursuing a course leading to an examination in May.

Now is the time to prepare plans to minimize the tendency for this situation to recur in the next academic year. A firm attempt must be made to make the extra year different from the preceding years. This will not be achieved by the renaming of courses containing material only slightly different from those in the third year. Neither can it be achieved by constantly striving to 'entertain' the students. They must appreciate the year for what it is, or can be: an extra year of *work* designed to provide a transition from school to the adult world. This does not mean, of course, that the work must be boring or formal but it needs to be purposeful, demanding, relevant and conducted by people with enthusiasm. Perhaps most important, the student needs to see that the staff, jointly and severally, consider the courses important.

It is proposed that:

1. A far greater slice of our fiscal cake must be devoted to this area.

2. The faculties must devise courses suited to the needs of these groups and must provide staff of adequate expertise and enthusiasm.

3. Each faculty in the school must ascertain those pupils who are *non-examination for its subject areas*.

4. The head of upper school must collate the findings of the faculties, to identify those who are *non-examination pupils throughout*.

5. Guidance and help must be given to the staff who are setting up and conducting the courses bearing in mind that this type of work is new to many and that we have a number of probationary or inexperienced teachers.

6. The possibility of extending interdisciplinary studies must be examined.

7. Each course must arise from a genuine need and not from the availability of a resource, e.g. a teacher, a room, a 'spare' set of students or a television programme.

8. Some courses will be more successful if held for a term or even half a term.

9. For some projects a different, more flexible splitting of the day will be needed.

10. When courses have been planned, consideration must be given to the overall picture :

(*a*) students must be allocated to courses according to suitability rather than availability;

(*b*) staff should receive similar consideration;

(*c*) the possibility of rapid alteration in the composition of the class and course must be 'built-in'.

School policy, like politics, is the art of the possible. Before the staff meeting discussed the proposals, the headteacher presented them with the staffing situation for the following year, and indicated that he had 'nothing up his sleeve' to meet proposals for new courses for these pupils. Indeed the total forecast of teaching-period requirements for the next year, based upon allocations already agreed in broad outline, matched within 1 per cent the teaching-period availability. New schemes had to be met either by a more stringent review of these allocations, or by staff agreement to modify the reasonably generous, but by no means excessive scheme of allotting non-teaching periods.

Immediately after the writer of the paper had presented it, with commendable brevity since it had been published in advance, the head of upper school gave some indication of the proportion of the year population for whom the present curriculum was, in his view, irrelevant, wholly or in part: 20 per cent of the year were either Easter leavers or taking at most one or two C.S.E. subjects. This was likely to be a regular annual percentage. It might even prove to be an underestimate.

Not surprisingly, reactions were varied. There were those who held that their syllabuses had been devised to be relevant to the entire ability range, and that the disaffection to school in general of this group of pupils did not vitiate their work. There were others no less vehement that their syllabuses could never be made relevant to this group: 'subjecting them to an eleventh year of failure for four periods a week' as one maths teacher put it. Some, speaking on general educational grounds, were against what they regarded as segregation of low-ability or poorly motivated pupils: 'a return to streaming, a departure from the principles of the comprehensive school.' Others did not see how one could possibly devise interesting integrated schemes of work for these pupils if their school day was fragmented by continual period changes, nor could they see how this fragmentation was to be avoided since it met the needs of the great majority of students.

No staff meeting in a large school could be expected to reach conclusive decisions in a matter as complex as this. In the three-form-entry secondary-modern school in which I began teaching I think it was just possible, though we were not then presented with issues so likely to produce situations of conflict of educational practice and philosophy. Fifteen of us were able to discount each other's idiosyncrasies and to pay due heed to the experience of weightier members of the staff. Anyway, we knew each other far better; teachers did not move every few years. Today a majority of secondary schools have more than 800 pupils, and teaching staffs of forty-five or more. There are many levels of involvement in decision-making, and we will be looking at these shortly. Whatever the structure a great deal of responsibility rests with the executive team for a balanced evaluation of staff opinion. It is plain that the staff meeting I have described could reach no conclusions by the exercise of a show of hands. The minutes merely show the consensus of opinion which the headteacher, as chairman, put to the meeting for approval at its conclusion.

Now the executive team's real work began. It had a mandate, as it were, to make practicable this general policy. This was to require repeated consultations with heads of faculties, singly and collectively, with groups of staff, in faculties and across faculties, and with pastoral tutors. On the production of a detailed plan to implement the policy, other decisions on the deployment of resources were to depend.

The composition of the executive team will vary from one school to another. In some it is the head and his three deputies. The Sidney Stringer School and Community College adds the administrative officer. Some schools include an elected staff representative, and the number which do so may well increase now that staff representation on governing bodies is becoming commonplace. Certainly a team is unlikely to function effectively if it is beyond a certain size: five or six at most. To counterbalance any feeling that the team is a cabal, it should regularly invite each head of faculty, for example, to meet it (regardless of whatever structure may exist for meeting heads of faculty collectively) so that it can listen to specific problems or suggestions, and receive a general progress report. Indeed, ideally, any member of staff should be able to ask to meet the executive team to present his viewpoint.

If it is to *act* collectively (and the rival merits of clear-cut role definition for each member and a symbiotic role definition for the team as a whole are argued in Chapter 3), it must take collective responsibility. Collective responsibility is a sham unless that collectivity is apparent to the staff as a whole. The head of Kinslade School asked two newly appointed deputies to write a 'no punches pulled' critique of the school as soon as they felt they had been there long enough to make reasoned judgements, but not so long that they had become absorbed in the system. They concluded it as follows:

> We also feel strongly that we need to look at ourselves, the executive team. We have to inculcate new enthusiasm downwards through senior staff. We must therefore decide where we are going and inspire in everybody confidence in our ability as an executive team. That means the establishment of a real team, without jealousies, accepting that the success or failure of one member is the success or failure of the whole team. Mutual help, advice, criticism is essential. We need to be much more united as a working body privately, and even more so in the public eye. It is important that members of the executive team teach in 'key' positions through the faculties. Where they succeed, they will inspire confidence in others. Even where they fail, they will have a valuable insight into the problems that face others.

The role of the staff meeting

The executive team must be directly responsible either to the staff as a whole or to representative bodies of staff, selective by virtue of office, elective, or both. It is widely held that when a staff gets 'too big' – whatever this may mean – staff meetings are a waste of time. Certainly when staff meetings are the occasion for head-magisterial homilies they are a waste of time, whatever the size of the school. But can staff meetings be made an effective part of the decision-making process even in a school where the headteacher sees his function as chairman, or indeed is prepared to surrender the chair to another member of staff? I maintain that they can. I would go further and say that I see no other way in which the staff as a whole can be exposed to the views of sections or individuals outside the mainstream, whether traditionalists or deschoolers. If a headteacher believes that a wide spectrum of educational ideology is vital to the creation of a dynamic school, then he must ensure that those who make up the spectrum have a voice. If he does not, factions will form and schisms develop.

The size of the staff is not over-important. We are obsessed with the idea that everyone needs to speak in order to be paid attention to. A member of staff in Kinslade School castigates staff meetings as a waste of time because 'only fifteen or twenty ever speak'. It is a chairman's job to see that certain wordy members of an already voluble profession do not monopolize the discussion, but one would counter this accusation with the hope that the rest are at least listening. In other ages, admittedly more leisurely or golden than ours, the forum and the moot were places of decision-making for groups often far larger than a school staff. What is important is the preparation for the staff meeting. It is wise to limit the number of topics, preferably to one main discussion, and to provide a working paper, as in the example I have given. Quakers ask members to come to their meetings for worship 'with heart and mind prepared'. There is much to be said for applying this precept to staff meetings. One might usefully quote further, this time on Quakers' attitude to the business affairs of their church: 'Give your whole attention to the matter before the meeting. If you want to speak, try to sum up what you have to say in as few words as possible. Speak simply and audibly, but do not speak for effect . . . Do not repeat views which you have already expressed . . . Listen as patiently as you can to all other points of view.' The main limitation that applies to meetings of a large body of staff is that they must be content to leave the detailed, needle-and-thread work to others. Staff meet to determine policy, but in the broadest sense. They must not feel railroaded into decisions. Only on very clear-cut issues is a vote a constructive way of deciding on policy. More often voting is schismatic, since, like opinion polls, it cannot take account of shades of meaning or degrees of commitment.

There are two alternatives to the staff meeting as a policy-making body. The first is that already indicated in the Portslade School Management Committee which entrusts responsibility to a named group of mandatory members, but provides for the ready admission, with equal rights, of all other members of staff. The main danger of this structure would seem to be that the mandatory members might, by the continuity of their attendance, dominate the decision-making. However free the elective members are to attend ('elective' indicates that they have this choice, not that they represent anybody), it is unlikely that they will make more than a peripheral impact on the formulation of policy. In Kinslade School, on the other hand, most but not all staff meetings are designated *staff open meetings*: staff may then come or not, as they wish. Obviously failure to come deprives members of staff of the right, morally at least, to criticize decisions taken. Attendance rarely falls below 80 per cent, probably little different from that of the traditional staff meeting after 'apologies'. At least people can decide that they have something better to do, if they wish, without the embarrassment of fabricating an excuse for non-attendance.

It is at the next level of decision-making, not the making of policy but the formulation of procedures that will put that policy into effect, that the idea of committees open to any interested member of staff may prove to be more practical. Here the targets are more specific. There is a strong likelihood that members of staff will come, not to be a part of the power structure – a possible abuse of elective attendance at the school management committee – but because they have strong feelings on the matter before the committee, or ideas which they are anxious to present personally. Kinslade School will again give us a clear example. The decision-making structure has evolved into that shown in Figure 15. The staff open meeting, as the policy-making body, is the nucleus of the structure. However important the other functionaries in the school may be, they are subordinate to the decisions of the staff. *This includes the headteacher*, save for his right to apply a veto to any decision which is in direct contradiction to the mandate given to him by his employer, the county or metropolitan district council.

The first staff open meeting of the autumn term decided that the school had been long enough established as a comprehensive school to look critically and objectively at *work standards*. It established from a list prepared for it by a member of the executive team an order of priority for discussion. It delegated to its two sub-committees, the Pastoral Committee and the Curriculum Development Committee the powers of decision-making that would implement its simple policy resolution:

'This staff meeting requires that, without in any way lowering our level of concern for the individual child in the school, steps be

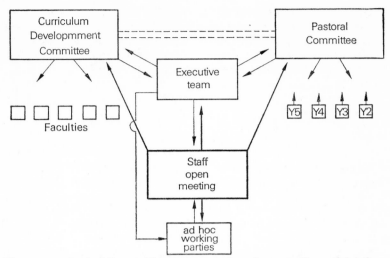

Figure 15. A decision-making structure based on staff participation: Kinslade School

taken to raise the level of academic achievement until it more nearly equates with the potentialities of our pupils.' The executive team took the view that the two sub-committees were so intricately involved in all aspects of the task assigned to them that it was futile for them to meet separately. Accordingly a succession of joint meetings followed, attended by a large number of staff who came by choice, some to all or nearly all the meetings, most to the topics about which they felt strongly. At each meeting a separate topic was the main item of the agenda:

Homework. Compulsory or voluntary? If compulsory for certain groups (e.g. examination candidates) and not others, how to justify differentiation in a comprehensive school? If compulsory for all, how to enforce, particularly where home conditions are known to be difficult?

Detention. To be used as a work sanction, not for behavioural problems. How can we ensure that failure to work is not fundamentally a pastoral problem? What lines of communication between curricular and pastoral staff? What of the pupil with a backlog of detentions? Parents who 'refuse' to allow children to stay in? Inequity of punishment between those who live nearby and those who have an irregular bus service?

Use of tutor group time. How can this be used to raise work standards? What is the tutor's professional position when he finds that a colleague is failing to set or mark work? How can we ensure that all tutors use this to good effect?

Assessments. Is the value of half-termly assessments commensurate with the effort required? Is it possible to devise a system which will give tutors, especially of fourth- and fifth-year pupils, a prognosis of exam performance? Should effort be indicated as well as performance? How are under-achievers to be identified?

Problem pupils. How do we cope with behavioural problems that are beyond the capacity of staff to deal with in the normal classroom situation?

In-service training. To what extent does the large school need a formal structure for helping its newly qualified (and newly appointed) staff? How far is this the role of senior curricular staff? Senior pastoral staff? One of the deputies? Should there be a specific appointment of staff tutor?

When the meeting had formulated its objective for each topic, it became the task of the executive team, sometimes working in consultation with staff appointed by the meeting, to specify the means by which that target might be achieved. Sometimes the steps taken were capable of objective evaluation. 'Had the scheme for half-termly assessments satisfactorily identified the under-achievers? Was there any evidence that it was acting as an incentive towards improved work standards? Had any unnecessary bureaucracy crept into the procedures?' In other instances the success of recommendations could only be measured subjectively: 'Were new staff more identified with the policy of the school? Was the need for punctuality at registration now better understood by all staff?' In both cases the success or failure in attaining the objectives set in previous meetings came under regular review.

After three months the joint committees were in a position to report back to the staff on its mandate, and the staff as a whole to decide whether the policy it had resolved upon had been put into effect. It would of course be a year or more before anyone could evaluate whether the labours of the committees had in any way achieved the desired end.

Union views

A number of different structures of management have been elaborated in this chapter, all of which in different ways contribute to the development of consultative procedures. Although the shortcomings of some have been pointed out, it is important not to think of some as 'right' and others 'wrong'. What is appropriate to one school in its particular stage of evolution is not necessarily good for another. Nevertheless, teachers' unions have spent much time recently formulating their policies on consultative and decision-making procedures. Presumably each association wishes its policy to become mandatory for all schools. The National Association of Schoolmasters[1] advocates the establishment of an academic board, as proposed for colleges of education in the Weaver Report[2] and now current practice in these institutions. On the academic board certain staff would be members ex officio and others would be elected into membership by their fellows. The Assistant Masters' Association and the Association of Assistant Mistresses favour the election of a common-room committee, of which the headteacher would not be a member, which would have the power to make recommendations on policy. The National Union of Teachers advocates an elected staff council of which the head would be an ex officio member, but draws a distinction between consultation, which would require a headteacher to discuss policy with his colleagues, and participation, which would require him to be bound by their decisions. It did not, as an executive member of that union of long standing has explained, 'reach this position without a certain amount of anguish. The N.U.T.'s [1972] working party on this matter recommended to Conference . . . that the union should support participation in its fullest sense. However, the executive made the reverse recommendation, taking the view that the feeling in the membership was that N.U.T. policy should be to aim now for participation in the sense of consultation, with participation in its wider sense being relegated to some future and more distant goal . . . Conference voted by a large majority to accept the executive recommendation.'[3] This decision was reaffirmed by the 1974 Conference.

Until there is legislation which reconciles or adjudicates between these various schemes, the power to create or not to create consultative bodies rests with the headteacher. It is not impossible for the staff of a school to create an elected 'pressure group' even when the headteacher is vehemently opposed to consultation. What it may achieve in these circumstances is another matter.

[1] See *Management, Organisation and Discipline* (N.A.S., 1972).
[2] *The Government of Colleges of Education* (H.M.S.O., 1966).
[3] Arnold Jennings speaking to his paper 'The participation of the teaching staff in decision-making in schools', part of the proceedings of the Third Annual Conference of the British Educational Administration Society, 1974, and published in *Participation, Accountability and Decision-making at Institutional Level* (Further Education Staff College, Coombe Lodge, Blagdon, Bristol, 1975).

Conclusion

There can be no greater self-deception than to believe that the creation of a structure guarantees its performance. Decision-making structures are tools in school policy-making. They will be as good as those who handle them. Their effective use depends on the motivation of the staff. Motivation is a factor that lies partly outside the control of the school. It depends on the esteem in which the teacher is held in society. It depends on the extent to which the local education authority for which he works facilitates his personal life by the prompt and accurate assessment of his salary, by help with housing, by demonstrating regard for him as a person. It depends not least on his own attitude to his profession. The Houghton Committee in its report[1] was right to remind teachers that, now they were to receive the professional salary they had been denied for so many years, they needed in return to show a professional dedication at all times. Nevertheless, whatever the external factors, it is within the school that we must look for the establishment of the ethos and involvement which will give effect to its educational aims. We know how important it is for children to feel wanted. Without this security they will almost invariably under-achieve, and often be disruptive. We should not be surprised that staff are likely to respond in the same way. For them the feeling of 'being wanted' is both personal and professional. To be cogs in a machine, however outwardly efficient the organization, is unsatisfying and soul-destroying.

The structures elaborated in this chapter are, therefore, not cold techniques for making the school as an abstract entity work efficiently. They are intended to make the school into a functioning society, concerned about the individual, his performance certainly but his well-being above all.

A school is not a unit; it may be a convenient fiction in a telephone directory or an administrator's inventory, but the only unit in education is a human being.[2]

[1] *Report of the Committee of Inquiry into the Pay of Non-University Teachers* (H.M.S.O., 1974).

[2] John Sayer, *Times Educational Supplement*, 17 May 1974.

6 Communication:
the school and its immediate context

There was a time when the school had little need to communicate. Its rules were clearly defined, though often unwritten, largely unchallenged and rarely changed. Within the school, communication meant exclusively the passing down to staff and pupils of such information as the head thought appropriate, and the passing up of such information as he required. There was no great need to consider communicating beyond the school. The interest of the press was confined to the publication of the results of public examinations and the report of the annual speech day. Times have changed. The school is no longer a closed institution responsible only to an abstract academic idealism. A high proportion of the public money collected through rates and taxes is expended on education, and the public, properly, believes that it has a right to learn whether that money is being wisely spent. The school is thus accountable, and accountability demands communication.

Words change too. 'Communication' is one which has elaborated its meaning in recent years. It implies not merely the transmission of facts, ideas, opinions and decisions, but also the dialogue that is based upon facts, promotes ideas and opinions, and reaches decisions. Communication has therefore become an integral part of the process of management.

Staff communication

This chapter looks at the areas within the school where communication is necessary and examines the means by which it can be achieved. Appropriately it begins with the staff.

How can I obtain thirty copies of a piece of work I have prepared for my class? Is there a detention system? Who on the staff gives permission for a sick child to be sent home? What happens to the children on wet lunch hours? The answers to questions like these, pedestrian though they may seem, are of great importance to new staff,[1] not only because they may meet any of them on their first day, but because their confidence and morale will easily be undermined if they appear to vacillate, or to contradict what are to the children established procedures. A school needs a handbook for the staff in which all routine information

---

CONTENTS

I. SAFETY

Fire, Accidents, Medical room, Car parking

2. THE SORT OF SCHOOL WE ARE

Academic organization, Staff meetings, Control, Parents, Out of school

3. THE WORKING OF THE SCHOOL — STUDENTS

Attendance, Leavers, Exemption from lessons, Absence of students from lessons, Reports, Voluntary fund, Lost property, Books lent to pupils, Minibus, School journeys, Visits

4. THE WORKING OF THE SCHOOL — STAFF

Absence of staff, Courses and conferences, Timetable modifications, Professional associations, Staff-room committee, Assembly, Correspondence, Communication, Duty staff, Records of work, Student teachers, Student records

5. THE WORKING OF THE SCHOOL — FACILITIES

Lunch arrangements, Visitors, Telephone calls, Duplicating and typing, Office, Library, Film bookings, Careers, Equipment, Furniture, Damage to property

---

Figure 16. Kinslade School Staff Handbook

[1] *Why Wasn't I Told?* by Norman Evans (Blackwell, 1972) is one of the wisest books on communication and interpersonal relationships in schools that I have come across.

appears in an easily accessible well indexed form, but succinctly phrased. Kinslade School groups the contents of its handbook under five headings as shown in Figure 16.

Properly devised the handbook does more than tell the staff when and how to act. It also conveys something of the general ethos at which the school is aiming. A good example:

Control
We are trying for a rational society in which our students learn to care about their impact on other people and learn to know themselves and the quality of their effort. There is therefore no corporal punishment, no 'lines' or 'copying', no mere sending out of the classroom.

Any failure to do classwork or homework *must* be checked. To help you there is a system of lunch-time (Tuesday – Friday) and evening detentions (Wednesdays). The latter needs advance notice to parents, using F10.

The system is designed for catching up on work and is not just for 'punishing' bad behaviour. Details of how it works are to be found on the cover of the detention books in the staffroom.

Bad behaviour is best dealt with as damaging the school's ability to serve. Students can usually be made to see that they should give some of their time to do something positive for the school in compensation – but such 'service' must be checked on by the teacher involved.

Teachers in difficulty in a lesson may ring for the senior member of staff on reserve call. There is a rota by each 'phone.

Persistent difficulty should be discussed with the appropriate pastoral staff who may have a particular way of reaching the student. They may issue a daily report book, call in the parents or an outside agency, or take the problem to the Governor's Care Committee.

Nobody expects a new teacher to memorize a handbook from cover to cover; but he will be wise to familiarize himself with its general content before the first day of term.

Here will be found matters of established routine. Some, like those concerning the marking of registers, fire drill or the action to be taken in the event of an accident to a child, may be decided for the school by the local education authority or other outside agencies. Others will have developed out of staff discussion, and represent a consensus of opinion which has now become part of the administrative or organizational structure. It is important for a handbook to be regularly revised: for insertions and deletions; for obscurities to be clarified; and above all to prevent some routines becoming hallowed by tradition when their original purpose no longer exists. It is healthy, though sometimes rather shattering to the ego, to invite a teacher or group of teachers at the end of their first year in the school to comment on the handbook's shortcomings.

There is the need also for day-to-day information to be published to staff. Traditionally in many schools this appears on the staffroom noticeboard. Unfortunately very rarely is there a noticeboard large enough to contain all that is required (and by the application of Parkinson's Law, the larger the noticeboard, the greater the amount of information which will be pinned on it). Noticeboards should be reserved for more permanent information: calendars of events, lists of courses, names of union representatives, for example. In many cases the day-to-day information is needed by the member of staff *outside* the staffroom: the time of a medical inspection, the name and status of a visitor to the school, the details of a return required by an examination board. If he is not to clutter up his memory with these details, he needs them in more accessible form. A duplicated daily notice in the pigeon-hole of each member of staff, though expensive of paper and office time, is a far more effective means of communication. Because its production is centralized there is less likelihood of contradictory or ambiguous information being disseminated. A good secretary will notice duplications or anticipate problems and tactfully seek clarification. Notices need not, indeed should not, be the prerogative of the headteacher; but the notice should show the name or initials of the originator.

Every staff committee or working party should make its minutes available to the staff as a whole. When these minutes or memoranda are the documents upon which a decision by the staff is to be based, they should be distributed to all concerned in advance of the meeting, but not so long in advance that they will have disappeared when needed. Communication, however, should not be identified with the circulation of paper, as it increasingly is in our bureaucratic society. The divisional H.M.I. for the area in which Kemshire falls always seeks an early opportunity in any visit to a school to go to the staffroom. He claims, with some justice, to be able to judge the standard of the school better in fifteen minutes' observation there than in a day spent studying curricula, in reading schemes of work, lesson notes and so on. Headteachers would do well to give careful consideration to this claim. I suggested earlier that all policy decisions reached in the headteacher's study or in committee rooms were valueless unless and until they were accepted by the teachers in the staffroom, not formally but operationally. The extent to which decisions are being put into practice, and the strengths and weaknesses of those decisions when put into practice, can best be gauged from the general discussion that takes place in odd corners of the staffroom.

'Free' discussion, that is discussion in which people do not strike attitudes, take stands, become conscious of the effect they are having, or not having on others, rarely takes place in a group that exceeds three or four, unless the members of the group have developed over a period of time a considerable mutual understanding and toleration. Indeed discussions on a one-to-one basis are the most productive, provided they take place in an atmosphere of informality. Many years ago a headmistress of great experience and wisdom wrote: '. . . I deprecate the custom of sending for mistresses except in an emergency. It is a jack-in-office trick that creates the wrong atmosphere and often defeats the object for which the interview was intended. It is much better to drift along a corridor and pick up the person you want. The conversation is friendly and natural and apparently fortuitous . . .'[1] The main difficulty today is that in our large schools it would be possible to 'drift along a corridor' for a long time and still fail to achieve one's planned casual encounter!

When the first school of which I was headmaster opened, I horrified the 'elder statesman' of the common room by joining the staff at breaks and during the lunch hour. He was a very dear and kindly man, but he had taught until then exclusively in grammar schools, and it was his belief that a headmaster simply did not do this. It was not merely, he explained to me, that the dignity of my office required that I took my tea in private. It was also that – and this he put with the utmost diplomacy – members of staff may wish to say things that they would not wish the headmaster of the school to hear. 'What', I asked him, perhaps a little disingenuously, 'could they possibly want to say that was for the good of the school but not for the ears of the headmaster?' He was not won by argument, however. It was the fact that my secretary, who brewed their tea, would also have to spend time separately making mine that persuaded him, since he was a man who would never knowingly put anyone to unnecessary labour. However, for some terms he still remained ill at ease at my presence until he saw the value of it personally and for others. Although he did not live to read Ronald King's description of ritualistic authority, he would have recognized that this was the mould in which he was,

[1] Dorothea Hiley, *Pedagogue Pie* (Nicholson, 1938).

from long-ingrained habit, casting my leadership role; the mould
which I was instinctively, and not then with any formulated ideas
on structures, seeking to break. Today there are few comprehensive schools whose headteachers segregate themselves from the
staff, and very many in which the positive advantages of being
available for 'casual encounters' are recognized. Unlike Miss Hiley
in *Pedagogue Pie*, I find that both in the staffroom and around
the school I have little opportunity to 'pick up the person' I want.
More important is that other people can chance on me.

'Chance' is a most appropriate word. No amount of planning
can ensure interpersonal relationships. As a headteacher of more
recent vintage than Miss Hiley has wittily put it[1]:

> If there is a nice, neat solution to the problem of internal communi-
> cation in the big school, we have failed to find it. In the beginning
> I was so afraid that in this large community nobody would know
> anybody that I think I aspired naïvely to a state of affairs in which
> everybody would know everybody – which, Hell being other people,
> is absurd.

The accessibility of the headteacher and other senior staff is
crucial to two-way communication. Good secretaries are rightly
protective of their employers, but they should never be a barrier
between the head and any member of staff who wants to come
and talk with him. Channels of communication are important,
but the reasons for departing from them may be even more important. When he has devolved upon others the power of making
decisions, the headteacher needs to be particularly vigilant to
ensure that he is not being used to override someone else's decision
or is in some other way being manipulated. With this proviso, he
should be freely accessible. By no other means is the mystique of
office likely to be more quickly and beneficially shattered.

The headteacher must be accessible not only to staff, but to
staff representatives. Many large schools have a common-room
committee, responsible in the broadest sense for the well-being of
the staff. At one level, this committee will concern itself with the
arrangements for tea-making, cloakroom accommodation, the
welfare of staff who are ill and social events. At another level it
may make representations to the head, the governors or the local
education authority about the availability of housing in the area,
the need for more ancillary staff, or any matter which affects the

[1] B. F. Rice, 'Life and Times of the Admin Man, *Times Educational
Supplement*, 24 August 1973.

conditions under which teachers live and work. There are times when decisions made for the benefit of the school as a community impinge upon the working conditions of the staff: a decision that control of movement or behaviour in a particular area of the school necessitates an extension of staff duties, for example. A curious dichotomy of thinking can easily arise in such situations whereby staff can see the need for and even request the control, but protest against the consequential extension to their duties.

There is, as one might expect in an educational system such as ours, no clearly defined code of what a headteacher may require of his staff, except that contained in the Working Party Agreement on the supervision of school meals. Even that agreement contains, deliberately one suspects, much imprecision, leaving the detail to be worked out in each school. Goodwill is an important commodity in the running of a school. This is particularly so when any salary negotiation is taking place (and when is one not?) because it is at these times that the general dissatisfaction with procedures or offers leads to union factions in the common-room. Whatever bitter differences there may be among unions at national level, a school is obviously a happier place if there can be communication between union representatives within the school. In a few schools the common-room committee is so constituted that it includes all union representatives, and acts as a liaison committee. In some others, union representatives themselves are prepared to set up such a committee. In most, regrettably, unions act unilaterally. Whatever the situation (and in whatever direction his own allegiances may lie) the headteacher must be approachable by union representatives; and if he is wise he will anticipate areas of conflict by discussing likely union reactions with them.

Communication with students

In many schools communication with pupils, as with staff, means the dissemination of information. In a school small enough to meet corporately it is supposed that the notices before or after assembly achieve this purpose. There is no evidence that this is so. Indeed, the constant frustration of teachers with pupils who 'didn't hear the notice' is evidence to the contrary. The fewer and briefer the notices, the greater the likelihood that they will be heeded. When they are tedious, or precede or follow religious assemblies that are themselves tedious, pupils will simply switch off. Larger schools have to think of other methods. In some, notices are given over a loudspeaker system at a set time each day.

Now that the B.B.C. precedes its news broadcasts on some channels with catchy jingles, perhaps we shall soon hear of some enterprising headteacher who follows suit, with 'This is Do-Do-Dotheboys Hall! Time for the news, so listen all!' Childen in such schools tell me that their attention to notices is directly proportional to the control of the teacher. In some classes, they continue to talk, read or write as the waves of sound wash over them.

Whatever the system it is essential that notices irrelevant to the listener are as far as possible eliminated. If fourth-year pupils are subjected to a lengthy notice concerning only the first year, they will no longer be listening to information which *is* their concern. In a school which uses daily notices for staff, there is no problem. A section headed 'For announcement' can be included, and the tutor can eliminate from it what does not concern his own students. Furthermore, 'the following pupils have failed to return library books . . .' becomes 'Mary, why on earth haven't you returned your library book? You left it on the bus? Have you been to the Lost Property Office? Then go tonight! And see the librarian at break today and explain.'

It is axiomatic that the smaller the unit to which information is disseminated, the greater the likelihood of effective reception. On the other hand, the greater the number of staff disseminating the information, the greater the likelihood of misconception or misconstruction on their part; and nothing will prevent what is intended as a mild rebuke – 'The 1st XV beat Washley School 1st XV by 15 points to 9 at home last Saturday. It is a pity that we had so few supporters as this was an excellent game, played in a very sporting spirit' – from becoming, from the mouth of a rugby fanatic, a homily on all that is wrong with the affluent society in general and youth today in particular.

But if communication is properly a two-way process what of communication *from* pupils? This may be individual, collective within the school, or collective through a national organization. A headteacher who is prepared to listen to the representation of an individual member of staff, but not of an individual pupil, runs the risk of being called a hypocrite. It is true that some children will consider accessibility to the headteacher as an opportunity for scoring off an assistant teacher, but most come because they have a very real sense of grievance, however flimsy the grounds for grievance may eventually prove to be. The head and other senior staff are necessary safety valves. Obviously they will seek to reconcile teacher and student, but there will inevitably come a time when they are faced with a conflict between plain justice and professional loyalty. What then? What of the pupil who complains that he cannot get on with his work (there are some) because of the rowdiness of others in the class as a result of the teacher's frequent disappearances from the classroom? Or the girl who complains about 'that name' Mr X called her. (All teachers new to an area would do well to find out the precise local significance of certain words of opprobrium before they use them – or, better still, don't use them.) More positively, a pupil or a group of pupils may come with a suggestion or a request for information. When this begins to happen, it is surely time to consider building into the management framework a procedure which extends consultation to the pupils of the school no less than the staff. The form it takes is not of great importance, provided there is built into the structure a direct contact between the student representative and those he represents. In a school with a house system, tutor groups may each have a representative on a house council and that body have representation on a school council. In a year system, there would be a year council, with representatives on a school council.

The school council is of secondary importance to the house or year councils which lie nearer to the grass roots and whose effectiveness can therefore be more readily discerned by the pupils. Any new school, or any school proposing to develop student participation, would do well to allow the house or year council to establish itself securely first. There is indeed no reason why one house or year should not unilaterally establish a council in advance of other houses or years. With a house system, the pupils in other houses will soon wish to have their councils if they see that councils have a genuine role to play in the school's management structure. In a year system, a successful fourth-year council, for example, is not likely to be prepared to disband itself when the pupils enter the fifth year the following September.

It is essential that even though a council may be established unilaterally, either as an experiment or as a prototype, the staff as a whole are aware of what is happening and accept the implications. In one school, where there was no school uniform for senior pupils, a year council decided that it should lay down certain guidelines on what was appropriate wear for school. It was insistent that these should be guidelines and not rules, because it felt that rules were unenforceable, and also because it considered itself able, given time, to gain consensus support from the great majority of the year. Through inadequate communication some staff who were not tutors in that year, and who had therefore not been involved even peripherally in the discussions, began in class-room situations to exploit the council's decisions as if they were rules. This undermined the effectiveness of the council in two ways. First, it was in direct conflict with the principle of co-opera-tion, not coercion, which underlay its decision. Secondly, even more important, it gave the impression to the less community-minded students that their representatives were the lackeys of the staff. What part should the staff play in students' councils? I would suggest that it be as little as possible. Certainly a staff member needs to be there in an advisory capacity, either on procedural matters, since few pupils have experience of chairman-ship or minute-taking, or on tactics. A wise staff member will be as self-effacing as possible. Above all a student council must be taken seriously, must be listened to, even if it may seem to be venturing into deep waters. It is, it must be remembered, only articulating those feelings and attitudes which pupils may well have severally and far less constructively. Under some local educa-tion authorities there are now pupil-governors in secondary schools. They cannot play any worth-while role on the governing body unless they have a mandate from the pupils and this they can have only if they have communication with them.

I mentioned earlier the possibility of pupil participation through national organizations. These may be student organizations, like the N.U.S.S., the youth organizations of political parties, or non-political organizations like anti-apartheid, peace or conservation groups. Before too rapidly dismissing these as external trouble-making bodies, the reader would do well to look at Swedish practice:

> In Sweden the national union of school pupils, S.E.C.O., has a membership of well over a quarter of a million and seems to be acting with considerable maturity and responsibility. It is aided by donations from the government and the trade union council, and has, with government approval, devised and begun to put into practice a scheme for a council in each school representative of pupils, staff, parents, education authority officials and school ancillary staff.[1]

Involvement at this level, with national approval, can surely only enhance communication between students and their schools. It is worth noting that the S.E.C.O. school council includes representa-tives of the ancillary staff. Caretakers and cleaners, groundsmen, technicians, administrative and clerical staff are in far too many

[1] Cyril Poster, *The School and the Community* (Macmillan, 1971).

schools regarded as there for the benefit of the teaching staff and not as an integral part of the school's management system. Often 'communication to' means *instructions* and 'communication from' equals *complaints*. At the Sidney Stringer School and Community College, Coventry – admittedly, because of its multiple role, a more complex organization than most schools, and therefore provided with more ancillary staff – not only do ancillaries find a place on several of the management teams, but there exists an administration team consisting of the four senior ancillaries meeting with the executive team.

In other less formal ways communication needs to be established. Is there any reason why the staff common-room of a school should not be open to *all* staff, whether teachers or ancillaries? Daily notices contain much information of value to the caretaker or catering officer and staff, and should reach them too. But genuine communication means genuine involvement in the making of decisions which affect ancillary staff, and examples of good management practice of this kind are very hard to discover in our schools. One possible reason is that schools in this country have been starved for so long of sufficient ancillary staff to meet the needs of the complex administration that is required of schools.

Communication with parents

Communication between home and school has changed beyond recognition in the past decade. The school or l.e.a. injunction, 'No Parents Beyond this Point', exposed by McGeeney and Young[1] in the mid-1960s in respect of primary schools, has been eroded partly by a succession of excellent books describing good practice in both primary and secondary schools and partly by a realization by teachers of their changed role in society. The view that parents are, except as progenitors, an unnecessary evil in that they interfere with the process of education is fortunately nowadays rarely held, or at least rarely expressed.

The initiative in communication should come from the school, which has, or ought to have, the responsibility to inform parents fully of the process of education their children are undergoing. Just as there is a handbook for staff, there should be one for parents, distributed through the feeder schools if possible, to emphasize the continuity of education. 'The school prospectus' is a phrase which has suddenly come into vogue. Regrettably it has

[1] P. McGeeney and M. Young, *Learning Begins at Home* (Routledge & Kegan Paul, 1968).

all the connotations of the private school selling its wares to prospective parents. The state school's purpose is not to be competitive but to explain. Parents are anxious to know the answer to
such mundane questions as how to pay for school dinners, whether
their child may cycle to school, what physical education kit is
required, whether there is homework, what to do if their child is
absent from school, and many others. A booklet such as 'Joining
Kinslade School' is simple to compile and anticipates many
parental questions. It does not matter how long established the
school is or how many children from the family have previously
attended, this booklet should go to every new entrant. Similarly
each key stage in a pupil's passage through the school needs a
brochure of explanation: the choice of options available in the

Dear Parents,

Your daughter has chosen to follow a two-year course
in Child Care which may lead to a C.S.E. award.   We
are writing to ensure that you, as well as your
daughter, understand what the course involves, and
that you are willing to support her in her decision.
It is not simply a course in 'baby-minding' but
involves a good deal of written work and study of
books about child development, as well as practical
work on the care of babies and young children, their
diet and the making of toys and clothing.   We would
like to feel that when your daughter has homework to
do, or materials to collect and prepare (for example
a 'nature table' for the play-group), you will help
her, not by doing her homework for her, but by
giving her encouragement, perhaps advice, and sometimes acting as a willing audience.   This certificate
is based on <u>continuous assessment</u>, which means that
there will be no formal examination at the end of the
course, but instead all the work which is done throughout the two years will contribute to the final result.

Written work will be kept in a folder to be shown at
the end of the course, and a record will also be
kept of practical work.

There will be twice-termly assessments to indicate
whether progress is satisfactory.   If all is going
well, you will see this from our remarks on your
daughter's work.   If it is not, we or your daughter's
tutor will be in touch.

                                        Yours sincerely,

                                        Beryl Smith

third or fourth year; the procedure for entering pupils for public examinations; the opportunities of the sixth form. Letters informing parents of school outings and journeys are commonplace. Letters seeking to involve parents in the actual learning process are far rarer. Kinslade School Home Economics faculty does this excellently: as the letter on page 100 demonstrates.

Teachers have to tread a careful path between the use of educational jargon and talking down to parents. They also have to find some way of ensuring that their letters are read. The example given above required the parent's signature, because parental acceptance of its contents confirmed their daughter's choice of option; but over-use or abuse of this practice makes it self-defeating.

There are few secondary schools which do not issue reports, but there are great differences in the manner in which they do this. By far the most profitable manner is through report evenings. Here the parents of one year are invited by letter to interviews with their child's tutor. The letter of invitation carries a reply slip asking them to tick the period(s) 7.00 p.m. to 8.00 p.m., 8.00 p.m. to 9.00 p.m., 9.00 p.m. to 10.00 p.m. during which they will find it convenient to come and, if the interviews are over several nights, the night they prefer. They are then given a definite appointment. On arrival, they receive their child's report, so that they can study it before the interview, preferably with their son or daughter. During the interview, if questions arise which the tutor cannot answer – usually questions about performance or behaviour in a particular subject – the parents are referred to the head of faculty or another senior member of staff who is in attendance. Alternatively the tutor offers to make an appointment for another occasion with the teacher concerned. Attendance at report evenings of this kind, *once the practice is established*, is high – in many comprehensive schools running at 70 per cent to 80 per cent. The burden on the tutors is considerable: with ten-minute interviews, twenty sessions can mean nearly four hours' work. The value of the personal contact established in this way makes it well worth while. Of course there are complaints and arguments; but these are better in the open, since the same complaints, often in a form far less amenable to reply, will still be voiced whatever the system.

'What about the 20 per cent to 30 per cent who don't come?' is a question frequently asked. It is hardly a question, it seems to me, more a rhetorical excuse for inaction; but, taken at face value, it deserves a reply. A letter can be sent giving a further opportunity for an appointment, during school hours, and possibly with a more senior member of the pastoral staff; or a visit to the home can be made, if this is acceptable to the parents; then, if all else fails, the report has to go home by post, with an invitation to the parents to come and discuss anything in it which gives them concern.

It is impossible to overstate the value of person-to-person contact in building a bridge from home to school. All the writers on home–school relationships have pointed out that parental memories of their own schooldays create a barrier which for many is broken down only by long and patient work by the school. When the report evening becomes also a social occasion, with tea or coffee available, pupils' work in evidence, committee members of the P.T.A. circulating freely, encouraging parents to talk and offer their services for projects which will benefit the school, then it may be considered to have 'arrived'.

Displays of work will communicate to the parents, their friends and the public at large the standards of work of the school. The school must decide on its purpose here. Is the exhibition a shop window of the best items of work, or a representative sample? The former approach may publicize high standards of performance, but it is likely to do so to the glorification of the most able students at the expense of the less good work of the trier; and the trier may well be less inclined to try in the future. The creative arts lend themselves best to displays: art exhibitions and fashion shows in particular. Science fairs are becoming popular, and these have the advantage of employing pupils extensively in conducting experiments and explaining to visitors the educational purpose of what they are doing. English has its shop window mainly in the new-style literary magazine, which in many schools has replaced the tedious reports of long-dead events that filled the pages of the school magazine. The humanities can publish reports of environmental studies, or mount exhibitions displaying three-dimensional work, film, colour slides, tape-recording, etc.

The school will do well also to look outside its own premises and resources for the opportunity to show its achievements: county agricultural shows, public libraries, pubs and shop windows. These are the subliminal ways of extending the community's understanding of curriculum development. More direct approaches – for example, lectures and demonstrations of modern mathematics teaching methods – though they will attract fewer people, are still important as means of communication. It is too seldom realized that the surest way to extend parental understanding of curriculum development is through their children. In our enthusiasm for new content or method, we as teachers fail to realize that the children, who have no yardstick against which to judge their present experience, do not have an instinctive understanding of the superiority of, say, integrated science to what it has replaced. For them it will be, unless we deliberately set ourselves to look at it through the eyes of the consumer, just another school subject. For their parents, consequently, it will be just another new-fangled educational gimmick, engendering antipathy and alienation. The school must translate the professional language of Bloom's *Taxonomy of Educational Objectives*,[1] into Wordsworth's 'the every-day language of men'.

Parents and the public are in all probability even more concerned about how a school is run than about what it teaches. Many schools which welcome the communication established through special events are still chary of an open-school policy which genuinely enables parents to see what is going on. Most of the rumours of ill-discipline in our schools are answerable only by the invitation, 'come and see for yourself'. A school which is not prepared to extend this invitation is open to the charge that it has something to hide. Of course every school which issues such an invitation runs the risk that visitors will at times see situations which one might have preferred them not to see. However, they also have the opportunity to see how these situations are dealt with. It is almost certain that whatever they see is nothing compared with the tales they have heard! Nevertheless, the open-school policy is not one to be embarked upon without a full understanding of its implications. For many teachers exposure to their colleagues in team-teaching situations or open-plan areas is a traumatic experience. To add to this unthinkingly exposure to the public at large would be poor educational management. The policy and its implications require no less discussion and planning than any other educational innovation.

Finally, a school must consider the role of the Parent Teacher Association as a communicator. The stated aims of most P.T.A.s will be modelled on the constitution drawn up by the National Federation of Parent Teacher Associations. Those of Kinslade School read as follows:

[1] Bloom, B. S., *et al.*, *Taxonomy of Educational Objectives: the Classification of Educational Goals*, Handbooks I and II (Longmans Green, 1956 and 1964).

The OBJECTS of the Association shall be :

(a) to encourage cooperation between the staff of the school, the parents and all others associated with the school;

(b) to encourage interest in the advancement of education both nationally and locally;

(c) to engage in activities of all kinds affecting the education and the welfare of all children attending the school.

It is essential that a P.T.A. is not regarded by the public as the headteacher's lapdog. It must be a critical body, constantly alert for ways in which the school is failing to communicate to parents as a body or to the individual. Few P.T.A.s are power-mad. If anything, too many are timorous of intruding on educational matters, and confine themselves to fund-raising and social activities. Valuable though this may be it is less important than the role P.T.A.s can play for the school as the eyes and ears of the community. Any institution which has illusions about the public esteem in which it is held, whether it is an industrial concern or a school, cannot lay claim to good management.

Communication between schools

In the past, the teaching profession has not had a good record for collaboration and communication between schools serving the same age group and particularly between educational institutions serving succeeding age groups. For this our competitive, selective system must bear considerable responsibility. At the same time it must be recognized that the eleven-plus examination formerly imposed on primary schools a far greater degree of conformity in content and method, and as a consequence there was less need for a close liaison over curriculum between the primary and secondary school. Today it is essential that the neighbourhood comprehensive school is aware of the educational objectives and the curriculum content of its feeder schools. It is also becoming increasingly necessary to see that there is a reasonable consensus among the feeder schools – if the transfer from primary to secondary school is not to be complicated and debased by weeks of revision to ensure that all the new entrants are in step. The headmaster of Paddington School, Liverpool once remarked at a conference that his pupils were drawn from seventy-four primary schools, and it was hard to establish a working partnership with so many schools from a wide geographical area. Most schools have a less exacting task. Nevertheless the increasing incidence of schemes with entry to the upper school at an age later than eleven – for example, at twelve to secondary schools in Hampshire, at thirteen to the upper school in the three-tier schemes, at fourteen to the community colleges in Leicestershire – makes liaison all the more necessary. In a growing number of areas teachers' centres are being used for 'bridging groups', so that the curriculum of the primary, middle or junior high school is co-ordinated with that of the receiving school. This means the surrender of a certain amount of autonomy in two directions: by the supplying schools which cannot afford, for the sake of the children, too great a divergence from the norm; and by the receiving school or schools which must be readier than some have been in the past to listen to what their colleagues have to say.

Visits of teachers from one school to another, better still exchanges for periods of a week or a term, do a great deal of good. No less important is the need for a link between the pupils of the different age ranges. In the main this is likely to be best achieved by secondary schools being of service to primary schools. Drama groups may produce plays designed for a younger audience. Sixth-year pupils as part of their general studies programme, or fifth-year pupils in the post-examination period, may give assistance in the primary classroom, on school visits, on the sports field, or in providing some piece of equipment needed by the younger children. The secondary school may act as host for the primary schools' athletics meeting. Collaboration through activity, and particularly through service, is the most effective form of communication.

It should not need saying – but it does – that where a number of secondary schools serve the same catchment area there must be collaboration towards common educational objectives and the promotion of group activities: co-operation rather than chauvinistic rivalry. Indeed I believe that some form of rationalization to ensure the best use of scarce resources is, in some areas of the country, essential to good educational management. In this respect Cambridgeshire is probably giving the lead with its consortia of 11 to 16 age range village colleges linked with one 11 to 18 college. If the practice proves to be as good as the concept, we have an unusual example of group management worthy of further study. Similarly the Stantonbury Campus scheme in Milton

Keynes,[1] in which three separate secondary schools are to share campus resources and work co-operatively through team management under a director, represents another departure from the normal unilateral management of secondary schools. Outside these formal schemes, there is still a considerable opportunity for the development among neighbouring secondary schools of joint curriculum planning and a common approach to both curricular and pastoral problems.

Schools and colleges

The links between schools and institutions of tertiary education have developed considerably during the 1960s though more to the benefit of staff as individuals through diploma and higher degree courses at institutes of education than to the schools themselves. More recently, however, a number of joint secondary – tertiary activities have been developing. Colleges of education have not merely used schools for teaching practice places; they have also joined with some schools in curriculum development projects, perhaps sending a small team of students of one discipline to reinforce staff resources. The basing of Schools Council and other national curriculum development projects mainly in universities, and occasionally in polytechnics and colleges, has created a useful bond between these two parts of the educational continuum. Linked courses for certain C.S.E. subjects, probably most extensively developed in Somerset and Kent, bring schools and technical colleges together. The remarkable growth of computer studies in secondary schools has led to a need to utilize the resources of colleges of technology and universities for this curriculum subject. In Kinslade School there is an annual art and craft evening at which a senior lecturer from a nearby college of art gives privately to the students his critical comments on the work displayed before the exhibition is opened to the general public. Most tertiary institutions seem to have become aware that they, like our schools, must shed some of their exclusiveness and mystique, and bridge the communications gap that has existed in the past.

Links, if they are to be meaningful, need reciprocal visits of staff and students. It is regrettable that many teachers regard school visits – which of necessity required alterations to the time-

[1] For a fuller account of the plans for the development of Stantonbury Campus, see the article by Geoffrey Cooksey in *Ideas* (October 1972) (Magazine of the Curriculum Laboratory, Goldsmiths' College, University of London).

table – as unwarranted interference with *their* classes, dooming all the pupils to instant examination failure: unless of course the visit concerns their subject, in which case it immediately becomes essential to the syllabus. There must be reasonable give and take over visits. It is true that the complexity of options timetables in the fourth year and above means that the absence of a group of pupils on a visit has implications for a large number of classes; but those who complain most seem to forget that even in a school with a high attendance in this age group, one pupil in ten is likely to be absent because of ill-health, holidays or truancy at any time. It is one of the tasks of management to ensure that visits out have a genuine educational or social value, that this value fairly equates with, at the least, the programme these pupils would otherwise be involved in if they did not go, and above all that there is full knowledge and discussion of these visits among senior faculty staff in good time before they are planned. Nothing is more frustrating than for a teacher to have ordered a film as a lead lesson for a particular phase of his scheme of work, only to discover that other plans have been made for his pupils.

Good management also ensures that staff appreciate the value of visits to the school of educationists, whether from other schools in this country, from advisers and inspectors, from representatives of other local education authorities or from overseas. Inevitably, new or experimental schools bear the brunt of these incursions. Countesthorpe Community College suffered a great deal in its early days from visitors wanting to see what could not possibly be, in a new school, there to be seen. Visits are time-consuming, and may make a disproportionate demand on the energies of the head-teacher and his deputies who are, after all, the members of staff most likely to be able to make themselves available, though not, it must be emphasized, by any means the least busy! None the less visitors have their value. Their questions and observations can, if the school's administration is self-critical, trigger off profitable lines of thought and enquiry; and visitors often bring useful knowledge of practice in other areas which provides a valuable link for the staff of the visited school. An aphorism to treasure is 'He who talks may learn from himself', and I find that when explanations of practice in my school are falling too glibly from my lips then that is the time when I need to be most self-critical.

School governors

The role of school governors is changing even as I write. The inclusion on governing bodies of representatives of staff and parents (and in some cases of pupils) and the selection by many county education committees of members with a genuine interest in the school, are healthy signs of a stronger community concern for education. In the past far too many appointments to governing bodies have been merely prestigious: the members concerned with their presence on the platform at speech-day and in the front rows of the audience at plays and concerts, rather than in the day-to-day running of the school. Local governors are likely to be the recipients of complaints and criticism from discontented parents. Good management makes them allies against misinformed criticism, by ensuring that they are knowledgeable about the affairs of the school; and it should not be difficult, where governors are assured that the senior management of the school will genuinely investigate complaints, to establish a procedure whereby the first question governors ask the complainant is 'Have you been up to the school?' In this way, far from the abhorrent nosy-parkers that some headteachers secretly consider them to be, governors can be an effective filter against rumour and false information, as well as a valuable channel of communication for the parent or child with a definite grievance. The relationship of the headteacher with his governing body is clearly laid down in his articles of government, complicated now by the fact that the headteacher may, in some authorities, himself be a member of his own governing body. Although, as a result of the Weaver Report,[1] principals of college of education are automatically and by right members of their own governing body, the practice of local education authorities, even after local government reorganization, varies widely. It is regrettable that there was not a similar report for the government of schools. We even have the ludicrous situation – where heads of secondary schools have the choice of taking up membership of their governing bodies if they wish – of one teachers' association (the N.A.H.T.) advising its members against and another (the N.U.T.) advising in favour, both supporting their contentions with the opinions of their respective legal departments.

The school and the inspectorate

Finally, there is the role of the local education authority's advisers and inspectors as part of the communications network within the educational system. 'Those who can, do. Those who can't, teach.' This snide comment on the teaching profession has been extended, presumably by teachers, with 'And those who can't teach, advise'.

[1] *The Government of Colleges of Education* (H.M.S.O., 1966).

There was a time when advisers and inspectors had themselves done little or no teaching; and it is inevitable that some will be called upon to advise in areas of learning or for age groups in which they have no direct experience. Many, however, are successful teachers who have seen the advisory service or the Inspectorate as a means, not of escaping from the classroom, but of making more widely available their skills and knowledge. They regard themselves as facilitators of the school's policy, rather than arbiters. There are times when on the education authority's behalf they have to moderate between contesting claims for resources, and as a result are likely to have at least one dissatisfied client; but most regard it as their role to achieve the best for the schools in their area, once they have satisfied themselves that the case is valid.

Increasingly local advisers have become responsible for running the many short courses, exhibitions and evening lectures and meetings that take place at residential colleges like Hertfordshire's Offley Place and Kent's Eversley College, at teachers' centres and at polytechnics, universities and in schools themselves. In-service education grows in importance as educational change accelerates. Although it begins within the school, it would soon become sterile if it were not matured by contact with ideas from other schools and the inspiration of educationists outside the schools. Much of the best work done by advisers and inspectors is in the creation of workshops for the communication of ideas. It is important that the planning of an education authority's courses should be influenced by representatives of teachers, and that those representatives have direct contact with the schools so that the advice they give is based on the needs of the teachers. The involvement of teachers in the running of their own schools must be extended, where this is not already the practice, to the management of teachers' centres and other places of in-service education. Most local education authorities' advisers both welcome and promote this relationship.

7 Communication:
public reputation

A school's concern with public relations is not confined to its defence from the onslaughts of the press when some sensational incident becomes 'newsworthy'. On the contrary, public relations must be viewed positively. Relationship with agencies outside those immediately connected with education, and particularly relationship with the community at large, are crucial to the reputation of the school. Indeed a school which has built up for itself a sound public image is likely to be more able to minimize the harmful effect of rumour, distortion of the truth and the antagonistic presentation of the facts which few schools today have not at some time experienced. The phrase 'public image' may grate upon the ear of some readers. It smacks of media promotion, self-aggrandisement, advertising. Undoubtedly there are times when schoolteachers would dearly like to be left alone, to get on with the job of education. The Newsom Report states, 'The less any school is an island the better. If it is to serve this generation it needs to be joined to the mainland of life by a causeway well trodden in both directions.'[1] If these words have any validity, we must accept the implication that our activities will be far more exposed to the public gaze than they used to be.

Social agencies

Every school is enmeshed in the intricate network of social agencies, both statutory and voluntary. The implementation of the Seebohm Report[2] has simplified the task of the school in respect of its relationship with the social services, even if the consolidation of

[1] Central Advisory Council for Education (England), *Half Our Future* (H.M.S.O., 1963).
[2] *Report of the Committee on Local Authority and Allied Personal Social Services* (H.M.S.O., 1968).

many diverse welfare and social responsibilities has not yet been satisfactorily achieved. Acute shortage of trained personnel, and particularly of resources, inhibits the social services from developing more fully the preventative role which would make less necessary the need for involvement, often coming too late to do more than patch up the damage in critical situations. Sad to say, in far too many parts of the country, particularly the inner urban areas most under stress, there is a lack of mutual trust between the two professions.

In most authorities, the education welfare officer is the link with the social services. Too many people, even too many teachers who should know better, regard him as a truant catcher and nothing more. Ask around in the community, and you will still hear him called 'the School Board man' a description which originated with the setting up of School Boards at the beginning of the century, and ended long before most of the parents who use the term had themselves begun to attend school! Titles, and the popular concept of the role of the title-holder, die hard. More recently he was called the school attendance officer. Though this more explicitly defines his main function, it does less than justice to the way in which he strives to ensure school attendance. It may be necessary for him to support a deprived family with the means at his disposal through the Education Department: free meals, clothing and travel grants, maintenance grants to enable the children of low-income families to continue at school beyond the statutory leaving age. He is indirectly concerned with the health of the child, particularly when ill-health, physical or mental handicap deprives him in some way of normal schooling. Inevitably he will encounter cases of neglect, family breakdown, severely abnormal emotional stress; and he may on these occasions judge that there is need of greater expertise or resources than he himself can command. These are the same children that the school sees – in the case of school phobics and truants, does not see. Their parents are those with whom the school also has dealings. The results of the education welfare officer's enquiries, or of the work of the social services department when it has become involved, are of crucial importance if the school is to play a supportive or rehabilitative role. Furthermore, because of the high incidence of social problems today, a primary function for the school may be to identify children at risk, and often to discriminate between those in more immediate need and those whose problems can be resolved without calling upon outside agencies.

Because the school is involved, then, in an area where there can be no clear demarcation of function, there is a danger that toes will be trodden on and feelings hurt unless we establish as part of the management structure of the school sound lines of communication with the outside agencies. There are three main principles.

The first is that communication must be established in non-critical situations, so that relationships are built before crises. A regular meeting between the headteacher or a deputy and the education welfare officer is essential, and the opportunity should be taken to involve senior pastoral staff who can give and receive first-hand information about those in their care. Similarly, but inevitably less frequently, there should be a regular meeting with the area social services director or his local team leader. The latter will know of the possibility of children being affected by domestic situations in which he or his team has been involved. Though the details may need to be kept confidential from the school, the fact that the child is at risk need not. As confidence grows, so secrecy declines. After all both parties are concerned in their own way with the welfare of the family. From time to time both the education welfare officer and the representative of the social services

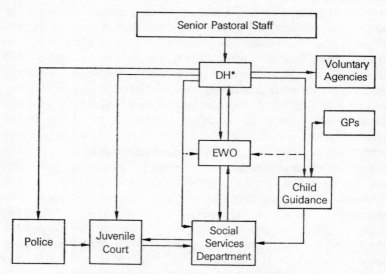

Figure 17. Communication network: social agencies

* In practice this may not be a one-person role; different 'routes' may well be the responsibility of different senior staff, including (in schools which have them on their establishment) counsellors or teacher/social workers. In such a situation inter-communication is no less important than communication.

department should have the opportunity to meet the staff as a whole. Obviously case-work cannot be dealt with in large groups. Nevertheless a greater understanding of roles and channels of communication can develop; and from generalized discussion staff may become better equipped to deal with welfare situations themselves and, even more important, to recognize the signs that indicate the need for reference to other agencies. This in-service education of staff should where possible be extended to include direct contact with these and other agencies : the psychologist or psychiatrist, on the role of the Child Guidance Service; the police or a member of the magistracy, on delinquency, for example. Some police authorities have appointed school liaison officers, for juvenile crime prevention, who are empowered, for minor offences, to give warnings rather than bring charges.

There are two ways in which there can develop a deeper involvement between the school and the social agencies, still in situations which have not reached crisis point. The first is again a form of in-service education for staff: a study of a problem child or difficult situation in which the members of staff most deeply involved meet with representatives of appropriate outside agencies in a case conference. We would do well to make more occasions in our schools for case conferences. We may be making inefficient use of our resources of time and energy by going around like bees, buzzing to all our colleagues about the problems this pupil or that is causing, when a policy of containment and treatment may evolve out of a more formal, planned discussion, with the benefit of expert advice. The second, more structured approach is that of the Care Committee. This evolved at Kinslade School as a subcommittee of the governors, though in other areas there are other ways of setting up this useful body. At Kinslade, it consists of the Chairman of Governors, six governors (two 'lay members', the two parent representatives and the two teacher representatives), the headmaster and the E.W.O. Meeting at least twice a term, it is able to look at general trends, see parents of problem children (or, more usually and more effectively, delegate this task to a small group of its membership) and call in the representatives of official bodies where necessary. This involvement of the governing body is in itself a valuable exercise in public relations. The governors' authority is beneficial to the school, particularly in those situations where staff feel isolated and vulnerable. The governors become more aware of the real nature of the problems facing teachers.

The second principle is that the school must be able to offer assistance as well as to require it. There will be times when, once good relationships have been established, the school is in a better position to give support than the social services. Where a good home–school relationship already exists, the intervention of the outside social agency may do more harm than good. More particularly, however, the physical and human resources of the school should be available. A caring school will know, for example, of potential foster-parents. It will be able to offer support to the elderly and housebound, leaving the Home Help Service (now a part of the Social Services Department) free for the most necessitous cases. It will assist in old people's homes, hospitals, with the mentally and physically handicapped. Many schools incorporate social service into the curriculum. Those which do so are likely to need to establish close links with the specialized voluntary agencies, like Mencap or Age Concern, or with the local churches, in order to channel their responses effectively. Whenever school pupils are involved in school hours in activities away from the school building, usually in small unsupervised groups, a school's public image may well depend upon the thoroughness of the planning. A woolly-minded, do-gooder approach may be counter-productive. For the pupils the activity must be purposive and, in the widest sense, educational. Simply to 'do jobs' is not enough. They must know the reasons why their help is needed; they must have direct contact with the organization and, where possible, the people they are helping; and when the task is concluded its value to society must be assessed if they are to gain any lasting value from their work. Parents, similarly, must be made aware of what their children are doing and why. Indeed, if social service activities are an alternative to other 'subjects' on the curriculum (as they often are for less able, unmotivated older pupils) parents must have the right of deciding whether or not their children are to be involved. Given a clear understanding that the activity is neither a soft option nor a way of eliminating problem children from the classroom, they are likely to support the activity. Often it can be shown that social service projects are based on an integrated curriculum: the skilful teacher will incorporate mathematics, English, craft work, social history and other subjects into the preparation for and follow-up of the activity. Where a sense of pride and achievement can be developed, the school will have gained immeasurably. The bugbear of all staff who plan off-campus, apparently unsupervised activities is that to the man in the street every child out of school is a truant. The issue of cards of authority, clearly identifying the task, the participants, the hours involved and the dates, goes some way to reassuring the public, provided they are prepared to enquire and not make rash assumptions. A number of community organizations committed under their constitutions to social service actively sponsor and assist with the running of school-based community service clubs. Rotary has its Interact clubs and the Lions run Leo clubs. Unlike their parent organizations the youth groups are not male preserves! Round Table, while it does not directly sponsor clubs, can be relied upon to contribute its resources of skills, time and energy to any social projects upon which a school may embark. Other organizations – Women's Institutes, Townswomen's Guilds, church groups of key members, conservation groups – are all valuable contacts for the school's overall educational purpose. Time spent by the head-teacher and senior staff in addressing their meetings on topics of their choosing is seldom wasted.

The third principle is that the school must build bridges within its own community so that its members – staff, parents and students – have a common bond and are less inclined to seek outside support. It is one of the sad consequences of our highly mobile, nucleic society, concerned with status and material benefits, as I have pointed out elsewhere,[1] that we do not know who our neighbour is. A school can act as catalyst. It may become aware of the existence of a handicapped sibling and be able to put the parents in touch with other parents who have learnt to cope with similar problems. Serious illness or bereavement may well come to the attention of the school more quickly than to any other quarter, the medical profession excepted. The school may be aware of family breakdown even before any other social agency. It is well placed first to help those involved in family crises to come to terms with a new situation, and secondly to offer help if help is needed. It is a truism that the existence in modern society of a complex structure of supportive agencies has reduced our capacity to cope with our problems and to respond to the needs of others.

Recreational and cultural activities

A school must make up its mind clearly about the educational and social objectives of its sporting activities, its plays and concerts. Like so much about a school, these are hallowed by tradition, not examined purposively. Naturally, any school wishes to excel on the sports field, but not, despite the poor example often set our pupils by the highly paid professionals, at the expense of sportsmanship. How far do schools see beyond this, however? The

[1] *The School and the Community* (Macmillan, 1971).

overriding aim of a physical and recreational education department in a school ought to be to ensure continuity of participation
of its pupils as they leave school. There are two ways in which
this can be done. The first is to establish links with local clubs,
encouraging them to cultivate and train young players with,
wherever possible, the help of the school. In a community school
this is far easier. The school has facilities for training which the
local clubs are anxious to use; and it is in their own interest, as a
quid pro quo, to undertake the absorption of young players.

The second way is for the school to act as a centre for locally
based junior and youth league teams. This brings it into direct contact with groups of parents, youth-club leaders and others who have
involved themselves in the organization of these teams. There are,
however, activities which are relatively new in both the school
and the community – Olympic gymnastics, judo and fencing spring
to mind as examples – which may have originated within the
school curriculum but for which there may be no adult organization to make continuity possible. Here one would think the school
has a specific duty to provide continuity by encouraging or even
establishing clubs for school-leavers. In doing so, often with the
support of parents, it brings pressure to bear on local authorities to
back up this provision. As a principle of management one should
always look at the school's recreational curriculum in the context
of what exists or what is felt to be needed in the community.

Similarly a school's cultural activities, particularly those plays
and concerts aimed at public performance, should have in mind
the tastes and responses of the audience. There was a time when
a school could rely on an audience for its activities, merely because
it was the accepted social practice for the parents to attend. For
many schools this is now a thing of the past. Productions and per-
formances must stand criticism at public level, and attract
audiences by virtue of their quality. That they can be a superb
shop-window for the school's cultural activities nobody would
deny. Regrettably they may also take charge of the school's main
educational function like a runaway carthorse, excessively absorb-
ing school time and resources. Well managed they will actively
involve a large number of pupils (not necessarily only the most
skilled), other members of staff, and parents.

Careers guidance and work experience

There are few areas in school management where role definition
is quite so confused as in the respective tasks of the school's careers

staff and the authority's careers guidance officers. The confusion is unnecessary, and derives in large measure from a lack of communication coupled with a certain amount of status seeking. Basically the school has knowledge of the student's abilities, potentialities and aspirations. It is likely also to know the parents, their aspirations for their child and the degree of support they will give. The careers guidance officers will know a great deal more about job opportunities, both locally and farther afield, and about long-term prospects. Both should know the various age and stage levels of admission into any industry or trade, and the educational requirements for admission, as well as the further education requirements after admission. Public confidence is rapidly lost if there is conflicting advice from the two parties to careers guidance. This may result from a false assumption on the part of the careers guidance officers about the quality of the student. A fifteen-minute interview is no substitute for the school's on-going relationship with a pupil and his family, though it may well raise a number of questions that will valuably be discussed with the school staff. Questionnaires and diagnostic tests have limited predictive value. Alternatively conflict may result from the supposition by the school's staff that their knowledge about careers is wider and more up-to-date than it is in reality. A great deal of time and energy is spent in some schools in making expert a number of its staff when that expertise already exists, outside the school but available for the asking. The presence of careers guidance officers at parents' evenings, the joint organization of careers conventions, and above all the ready availability to either party of information, go a long way to establishing students' interest.

Though many schools fight shy of recognizing it, there is also the employers' interest. This may be expressed in ways which the school deems to be interference with its curriculum. Nevertheless it is a public viewpoint, and it should receive consideration. It is possible that from where the employer sits there is validity in his criticism that the employee does not know his mathematical tables. What may be wrong is his assumption that modern mathematics is responsible for this state of affairs. Employers have much to offer the school. Approached collectively through employers' federations or the Chamber of Trade and Commerce, or individually through personal knowledge, or by way of parents or the careers guidance service, they can give invaluable direct help. For students in their last year at school work-experience schemes are now legal, and many employers are willing to involve themselves in the

detailed planning of these, and to make available their considerable resources. Personnel officers readily visit schools to talk to
pupils. With a little persuasion former pupils and parents will do
this too, and sometimes 'tell a plain unvarnish'd tale' that makes
refreshing listening. The school is not a vocational institution; but
its pupils and their parents look for a vocational end-product from
education.

The general public

It is a well-known fact that every misdeed of a school pupil is the
responsibility of the headteacher and his staff. 'One of *your* fifth-
year girls was drinking in a pub on Wednesday evening'; 'Over
the weekend a gang of *your* boys . . .', and so on. These girls and
boys might be thought to have no parents. It is tempting to refute
every complaint of this kind with a terse 'None of my business.
Out of school hours.' It is, however, salutary to reflect that if Mary
Smith rescues a boy from drowning over the weekend we will be
ready enough to recognize her as a pupil of our school and bask
in her reflected glory.

Somehow we must make clear to the general public in our
community that our concern for our pupils cannot extend to
jurisdiction over their every action. The standing of the school is
without doubt lowered by the antisocial actions of its pupils at any
time. If our homilies at assemblies have any sincerity, then we
cannot pass by on the other side. What we require, however, is the
active co-operation of the general public, the realization that
delinquency and thoughtless behaviour on the part of young
people is the concern both of the school and the community. Many
parents of secondary-school pupils, while ready to blame schools
for the lowered standards of behaviour, remain inhibited from co-
operating with the school by their own juvenile experience. There
is a perverse element of retaliation on the schools of this generation
for the authoritarian 'sins' of the schools of their generation!
This alienation can be broken down, though it takes time and
patience.

Perhaps the first prerequisite is the ability to listen to complaints.
Many complainants have a head of steam which they simply have
to blow. They have been offended, aggrieved, insulted, even
robbed or deceived. There is little to be gained in telling them from
the outset to take their complaints to the right quarter. The school
may well be able to help them discover what the right quarter is.
If an illegal act has been committed it is the school's duty to advise

the complainant of his rights in law. If the act is merely anti-social it may be that he should be advised to contact the parent. There are many times, however, when the school may wish tact-fully to influence the outcome. It may know that a child is from a deprived home, where contact with the parents may well be counter-productive. On occasions the intensity of the complaint may be out of all proportion to the alleged offence.

When the school shows that it is prepared to listen, then the general public begins to show a willingness to reciprocate. There are, for example, few cases of truancy that are not known about by neighbours long before the school is aware of them. While few members of the public wish to become known as snoopers, every-one knows that the law requires the parents of a child of school age and in good health to send him to school. If the parent is being deceived, neighbours do the parents no kindness in allowing the deception to continue. If the parent is condoning the offence, then it is socially irresponsible for anyone to ignore the situation. Truancy is cumulative. When it reaches, as it has done in many inner urban schools, a stage at which the school and the supportive agencies have no longer the resources of time and energy to enquire into suspect absences, then the pass is sold, and the school's control breaks down. Since the neighbours may also be parents and grandparents of schoolchildren they are sowing the seed of destruction for their own kin. Self-interest, no less than community well-being is at stake.

It is doubtful whether direct appeals to the public to help the school to combat truancy, vandalism, illicit drinking, and so on will produce much co-operation. First it is essential to develop an awareness that the school belongs to the community and that its students and their studies are part of the community. A positive policy towards community involvement is needed. For example, when there is a complaint about litter around the shops frequented in the lunch hour by some of the school's pupils, what better demonstrates to the public the school's concern: a lecture in assembly, or a fact-finding visit to the shopkeepers by a member of staff, followed by a litter clearance by volunteers? It may well be that a lack of suitable receptacles creates the problem. Then the school and the shopkeepers ought to join forces to press for better provision. What governs the number of litter bins in a parti-cular area and the frequency with which they are emptied? Per-haps the school might find a useful social education project arising from the comparison of one area with another. There are many examples of the change in public recognition of the school that stem from awareness that education is about real issues. Eric Midwinter's case for a community-oriented curriculum:

> the child is dignified by the acceptance that education can be about him and his environs, that he is an historical character in a geographical situation with social, spiritual, technical and other problems facing him[1]

is supported by the argument that:

> parental involvement and support for curricular enterprises would probably be enhanced . . . in that the parents' own experience, occupations, insights and so forth would be material evidence. The mysteries of the school would be, in part, replaced by a substance well known to the parent.

Midwinter would, I am sure, readily accept that the words 'parent' and 'parental' can be extended to 'community' and 'communal'.

The media

Education is news. Unfortunately much of the news about education is bad news. For this the media bear some responsibility. In its evidence to the Royal Commission on the Press the Inner London Education Authority wrote:

> Some recent interviews – not confined to the press – have caused the authority and its teachers concern. Typical examples have been: children kept out of school in order to be interviewed about alleged activities within the school, without permission being sought from school or home; children being interviewed in such situations as virtually to prompt them to make damaging comments; children's dramatic stories of situations presented as bona fide 'eyewitness' accounts, when investigation later has shown such accounts to be hearsay; the 'setting up' of children to pose for dramatic news pictures.[2]

Perhaps the worst example of the last abuse was when children were encouraged to re-enact for the benefit of the television cameras a scene of inter-racial violence that had allegedly occurred in an urban school.

Schools also bear a responsibility. They have been reluctant, often obsessively so, to co-operate with the press. Editors, particularly of the local press, recognize that what goes on in schools arouses public interest and sells copies. Reporters have a difficult job to do, with deadlines to meet, and they are not helped by

---

[1] Eric Midwinter, *Projections* (Ward Lock, 1972).
[2] Quoted in the *Guardian* (14 January 1975).

obstructive tactics on the part of the school's spokesman, usually the headteacher. The National Association of Head Teachers gives some sound guidance:

> Many of the problems that occur in unfavourable press reporting arise from the 'No comment' response of the person approached. This response is often dangerous since, when quoted in a press report, it tends in the reader's mind to confirm allegations made in the report. Even if one cannot . . . give a precise answer to a question, it is best to say something.[1]

The school must draw a distinction between matters which are genuinely *sub judice* and those which it would like to be but are not! A matter is not *sub judice* simply because the school may not come out of it in a good light. Editors will, in the main, respect honest dealing. They are not likely to support employees who fabricate or distort evidence. A school's relationship with a newspaper does not begin and end with the sensational incident. It needs to be built up over a period of time. Invitations to school functions, information of school successes, accurate facts and figures wherever possible, a helpful attitude of assistance to reporters who want to know about some general educational issue or want an off-the-cuff response to some 'wild-cat' political statement about education – all these build up a good relationship.

It is not necessary for the headteacher to be the only source of information to the press or to local radio. P.T.A.s often appoint publicity officers, and it helps the school if items of news are conveyed through a parent. Whatever the arrangements it is essential that when a news item is in the offing a prepared statement is ready, not to be followed slavishly but to ensure that the facts are fully covered.

A school has its own media resources. The school magazine, annually recounting successes and failures in long-past sports fixtures, bidding regretful farewells (six months in arrears) to 'Mr Bath-Oliver whose long and faithful service to the school . . .', is happily a thing of the past. Livelier, topical publications have replaced them. School newspapers, produced by students with the technical assistance of a member of staff or a parent, can lead to productive controversy and a feeling among pupils of positive involvement. Each school must, as a principle of management, establish its own attitude towards 'censorship' of contributions. Ultimately the headteacher will be publicly accountable for what is published. Obviously a school newspaper is no less open to

[1] *Council Memorandum on the Press and Head Teachers* (February 1974).

charges of libel, if it were to engage in damaging criticism of individuals, than any other publication; but this situation is most unlikely to occur. More frequently some statement is made or some topic aired that, within the school, will be clearly understood; but student editors tend to forget that there is no such thing as an 'in-newspaper'. It will be read widely by parents and others, and avidly seized on by the press if there is anything quotable. One of the first numbers of Kinslade School's newspaper carried a light-hearted 'investigation' by some students into the popularity of school meals. In fact the school meals were outstandingly good. Inevitably, however, the article carried criticisms, usually by those whose concept of a balanced meal would send shudders down the spine of any dietician. The school meals staff reacted indignantly and demanded the right of reply. The students of the editorial board readily gave it, realizing incidentally that they would have been wiser had they given it in the number in which the original article appeared, by showing the meals staff the copy in advance. The reply not unnaturally included criticism of student behaviour, waste and lack of helpfulness, though in general it was positive and more conciliatory than the students had a right to expect. None the less the criticisms of behaviour were picked up by the press, quoted out of context and given lurid headlines—an object lesson, if one were needed, that there are public considerations even in a domestic publication. With well-established relationships between students and staff, the editorial board will usually seek approval in advance for anything which might cause difficulties were it to appear in print. A headteacher ought not to seek to censor any statement simply because it does not accord with his views. The criteria for publication must be public decency, avoidance of hurtful, untrue or misleading statements, and balanced arguments in areas of controversy. The school newspaper can have a valuable educative as well as a social function.

School literary magazines have become increasingly popular and the standard of creative writing in them is encouragingly high. Any such publication will enhance the image of the school, though care must be taken that a disproportionate amount of the school's financial resources is not spent on something merely prestigious. There are two main dangers in school literary publications. Some are monopolized by cliques and become merely the preserve of intellectual mutual admiration societies. Others are little more than the final resting places of highly commended work from the English classroom.

Schools with broadcasting systems can establish domestic radio stations for lunch-hour broadcasts, with pop music interspersed with tape-recorded interviews and items of domestic news. Although in the previous chapter I was critical of the use by the headteacher of a broadcasting system for *his* announcements, I believe there is much merit in allowing students to set up a school radio station which can then be used incidentally for announcements and information. Skilfully presented, information about the school's next dramatic production can be broadcast repeatedly; and because our pupils are used to repetition in commercial television and radio the message is more likely to get across. Perhaps this smacks of 'If you can't beat 'em, join 'em.' There are worse policies in public relations!

The calendar of events that a school prepares each term can be a dry-as-dust catalogue, or it can be attractive and entertaining. The extract from the Spring term programme of Kinslade School on the following page surely comes into the latter category. A number of school events can with advantage be recorded in some way; visually on film, by photographs made into a film strip, on colour transparencies, even in some schools on videotape; aurally on tape-recordings or on records. The visual record of, say, a school exchange abroad is not merely useful for an 'after the event' meeting for parents of those who went. It can also be sent to the hosts for presentation there, and used as the basis for the next year's visit. A school which takes part in exchanges within a twin-town scheme may be able to act as a centre for the accumulation of a continuous record of the contacts made by various clubs and societies and by civic dignitaries. This is a most valuable contribution to local history and international understanding.

The importance of good public relations both for the school itself and by the school on behalf of the community is much under-estimated. No school ought to seek publicity simply for its own self-aggrandisement, or for that of the headteacher. Regrettably, there are some present and former headteachers who have set themselves up as Sir Oracle, and their schools as ideal institutions, evidence of the brilliance of their management, educational theory or charismatic personality. Modest reserve is not merely a pleasant social attribute. It is a wise precaution when today's boast may be tomorrow's burden. There is the danger that concern with the public image may improperly influence educational decisions, that communication will determine objectives. This stands educational management on its head.

Kinslade New Sheet

The first three months of 1976 are going to be extremely busy at Kinslade School. Would you like to know what is happening so that you can book some dates in advance? All meetings begin at 7.30 p.m. unless otherwise stated.

On Thursday, 15th January in the fifth-year common room a senior police officer is going to speak at a P.T.A. meeting on 'The Police in Kemshire'. It is easy to think of the police in terms of breathalysers and speed traps, but the role they play in our community is a vital one, and this should be a meeting of particular interest. Everyone is welcome – all meetings are open to anyone – and we particularly recommend this one to school and evening-class students of sociology as well as to the general public. (See also details of a talk on the Probation Service later this term.)

There are few people in Kinslade who have not by now heard of the tremendous successes of the Gymnastics Club. You have the opportunity to see these young people in action twice this term in a four-sided match in the school sports hall at 2.0 p.m. on Saturday, 7th February; and in the Gym Club Championships all day on Saturday, 24th March.

On Wednesday, 4th February we have a most original evening entitled 'What is a School Governor?' Most people know, vaguely, that all schools have governors or managers. But do you know what they do? The P.T.A. thinks you ought to, and a number of school governors have kindly offered to put on a mock governors' meeting to demonstrate.

On Friday, 13th February the Kinslade Art and Craft Association is mounting a display of the work of local amateurs, including a number of past and present Kinslade students, entitled 'The Seeing Eye'.

Conclusion

The main aims of communication in educational management can be summarized as follows:

to bring social cohesion to the organization;

to enable decisions within the school, whether on the treatment of the individual pupil or on major matters of policy, to be reached on a basis of sound information and not on prejudice, misconception or self-interest;

to enhance the public reputation of the organization, where good repute is deserved, and to encourage reasoned criticism where it is valid.

Channels of communication must be established, and this may take time and patience. There is need for structure, but excessive structure may create an over-formalized system in which personal responsibility is submerged and initiative stifled. Much within the field of communication, inside and outside the school, depends on a clear concept of the aims of the institution. Given this, immediate responses to situations will be soundly based and in the communal interest.

8 Techniques of educational management

There are four essential features in the introduction into a school of any innovation, and these are applicable equally to organizational change and to curriculum development.

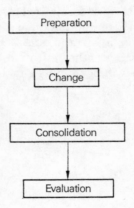

Preparation

It is necessary to be clear from the outset how the need for change has arisen. It may be determined by factors beyond the control of the school: secondary reorganization, increase in the size of the school population, or changes in the pattern of public examinations – the introduction of the Certificate of Extended Education, for example. It may arise as a consequence of other developments within the school, when one change triggers off another. For instance, the successful introduction in one area of the school curriculum of a Mode 3 C.S.E. syllabus may lead to similar proposals from another faculty; or a pilot scheme in team teaching may lead to a desire to see this more widely practised. These consequential developments may or may not have been foreseen at the time of the original innovation. The proposals for change may stem entirely from response to a new situation within the environment. A local firm may come forward with proposals for a work-experience scheme or the P.T.A. may present the school with a minibus. Finally, the innovation may be considered desirable in order to renew the school's commitment to its ideology or overall educational aims.

Part of the preparation must be to determine the kind of change required. To this end clearly defined objectives must be established. A set of loose-knit pious platitudes will do no good. It is dangerously easy to convince oneself that one has determined objectives when one has done nothing of the sort. Semantic precision is important to avoid 'Oh, I thought we meant . . .' situations. The objectives should come under keen scrutiny from those who will be engaged in the innovation. Time spent here will be time saved later. The main purpose of the sequence from preparation to evaluation is to ensure that the final stage gives a positive reading. If it does not, the fault *may* lie with the original definition of aims and determination of objectives, and the entire exercise is vitiated. (See flowchart, Figure 18 on p. 130.)

Time may or may not be of importance. Some innovations are open-ended in this respect. The change to mixed-ability teaching described in Chapter 2 is one example. Devising a scheme for a restructured option system is another. Provided the present system is workable it matters little whether the innovation, if introduced, takes places this September or next. In most cases, however, the timing of change will be important, since so many other features of the school organization may be liable to modification as a result of this innovation. A time plan is therefore part of the preparation. However arbitrary it may be to begin with, it is the framework on which to hang the decisions which have to be taken. It also, as will be seen in the section on critical path analysis, forces those involved in management to recognize the stages in decision-making towards a set of objectives, and to establish a sequential relationship between those stages.

Change

In one sense change cannot be separated from preparation, since those who are involved in the change must also be involved in the preparation. This involvement modifies their attitudes, and reduces the impact of the change. In the words of one headmaster-colleague, 'Change must be fed in from below.' Nevertheless, however thorough the preparation, the actual innovation has a character of its own. Exposure to the innovation, whether curricular or organizational, will produce unforeseen reactions and side-effects, from both staff and students. Now it is doubly important to keep the objectives in mind, lest minor diversions be rated as major disasters. Probably the greatest danger lies in the inability of those most involved to get out from under the trees so that they can see the wood.

The preparation must not be so uncompromising that it leads to inflexibility. There must be freedom for manoeuvre within the overall scheme. Flexibility must not be confused with vacillation, however. No innovation will be a success if it does not engender an air of confidence.

Consolidation

Just as preparation merges imperceptibly into change, so change blends with consolidation. As each piece in the structure proves itself, then it needs to be cemented into position. If there is need for modification in the materials, or the techniques with which they have been handled, then it should be noted or carried out. It may be that the success of a future stage in the innovation depends upon the modification being made there and then; but there is a danger in too much tinkering.

One must be prepared for failure. It is vital, however, to decide whether a particular failure is incidental or structural. One must also be prepared for success. We take a masochistic delight in our educational failures – perhaps a reflection of our inherent conservatism – almost to the point of ignoring our successes.

Evaluation

Perhaps the least happy feature of educational innovation is our reluctance to evaluate. We say defensively that it is impossible in education to create laboratory conditions, with control groups against which we can measure the success of our innovation. While this is undoubtedly true it is too frequently used as an excuse for inaction. Even subjective evaluation is better than no evaluation at all. Many a research worker has learnt a great deal from assessing people's attitudes and opinions, even though he may know that those attitudes and opinions may be based on ignorance, misconception or prejudice. Many teachers found *Enquiry 1*[1] hard

[1] *Enquiry 1: Young School Leavers*. Report of an enquiry carried out for the Schools Council by the Government Social Survey (H.M.S.O., 1968).

to accept when it was published. In particular it disclosed a great gulf between the importance that children and parents on the one hand and teachers on the other attached to various school objectives. Teachers failed to realize that it was not necessarily true that their values had been negated. What was obvious was that, whatever the reason, they were not shared.

Evaluation is essential if we are to make progress. Without it we are only playing hunches, and are likely to blow hot and cold as the mood takes us. Because much of our school-based curriculum innovation takes place without reference to others, it is possible that we miss the opportunity of monitoring our success and failure against performance in other schools. Particularly, but by no means exclusively, with Mode 3 C.S.E. syllabuses, a consortium of schools can produce a syllabus which still leaves each member-school considerable freedom of action. If, however, the schools in the consortium have agreed objectives and common evaluation techniques, the effectiveness of the way in which the syllabus has met those objectives can be judged comparatively.

A good innovator is a pessimist in preparation, an optimist in execution and a realist in evaluation.

Flowcharts

A flowchart is a simple method of monitoring the procedures from preparation to evaluation in logical sequence. Above all it pin-points the areas to be re-examined in the evaluation process.

The technicalities of flowchart notation can, for our relatively simple purposes in education, be reduced to these elementary rules:

1. Every chart must have a start point and at least one stop point, indicated by lozenges.
2. Instructions are shown in rectangles. There may be any number of inputs for an instruction, but only one output.
3. Questions are shown in diamonds. There can be any number of inputs, but only two possible answers, 'yes' and 'no'.

The flowchart is concerned only with feasibility. Is what we want to do capable of being done? What steps are necessary towards the doing of it? Having done it, have we achieved what we set out to do? A simple demonstration of a syllabus flowchart is shown in Figures 18 overleaf.

This flowchart contains the four stages in innovation, although, of necessity, the interplay between change and consolidation

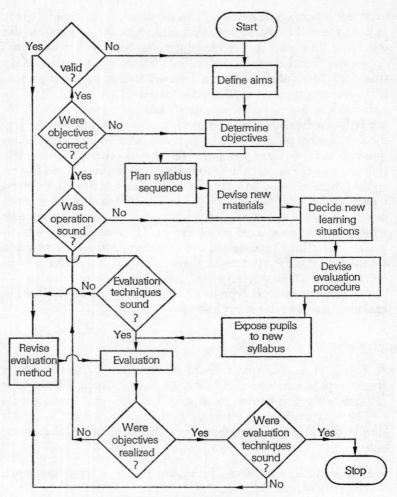

Figure 18. Syllabus flowchart*

* The final version of this flowchart, which combines skilled precision and aesthetic balance, is the work of Eric Franklin, Head of Mathematics, Buckhurst Hill County High School, Essex.

cannot be shown. In practice it is extremely unlikely that the learning situations will not be subject to continual modification as the pupils and staff are involved in the assimilation of the new syllabus. For example, if team teaching[1] is one of the innovatory

[1] For a detailed exposition of this technique, see David Warwick, *Team Teaching* (U.L.P., 1971).

learning situations required to meet the curricular objectives, it is not likely to spring ready-made from the mere conjunction of the teachers forming the team. Initially the team is likely to operate in one of two ways. Either it will have a leader and sub-ordinates, so that the brunt of the planning and exposition falls to the lot of one member of the team; or the members of the team will perform independently, though they may be collaborating in the preparation of materials. Gradually, as mutual confidence is established, the leader-led role concept implicit in the first example may become eroded and the leadership depend not on status but upon the skills that a particular member of the staff has to offer at any given stage of the syllabus. In the second example, the benefits of collaborating over the preparatory phase may encourage colla-boration in the expository phase.

Similarly it may be found that the failure of one stage in the syllabus sequence has its effect on future stages. No sensible person waits until the evaluation to remedy this deficiency. The soundness of the operation needs to be monitored constantly.

Critical path analysis

Critical path analysis is a relatively new technique in business management, unheard of in any form until twenty years ago, and under its present title and in its present form until ten years ago. It is erroneous to think that it is a technique to be used only with large projects, or that it needs to be used always in conjunction with a computer. It is a relatively simple technique for forward planning, invaluable when there is the need to work to a deadline. Indeed the word deadline sums up the essential quality of C.P.A. Whereas flowcharts are concerned with feasibility, C.P.A. is con-cerned with the timing of operations.

New as C.P.A. is in business management, its application to education is only just beginning to be considered. So far use of it has been more by educational administrators than by schools themselves. There is no reason why its use in schools should not become widespread. It is logical in its construction, susceptible to modification, applicable not just to the school which sets up the network but to any school which shares the same temporal restraints.

In business management C.P.A. 'can be used in situations where the start and finish of the task can be identified'.[1] In educa-

[1] This quotation, and the terminology used throughout this section, come from K. G. Lockyer, *An Introduction to Critical Path Analysis* (Pitman, 1969), a clear, methodical explanation of this branch of cybernetics.

tion we are very much bound by crucial end-points – examination
dates, ends of term, last dates for staff resignation, for example.
For us therefore the value of C.P.A. may sometimes be that we
can work back to identify the start-point. Put simply, in civil
engineering C.P.A. may answer the question 'by what date can
the motorway section be completed?' In education it may ask the
question 'when do I have to begin to ensure that everything is
ready for the fifth-year Parents' Evening?'

In the previous section we dealt with the feasibility of the introduction of a new syllabus. In this I will take as my first example
the introduction of a Mode 3 C.S.E. syllabus. There are three
distinct areas of decision-making which are controlled by the time
element.

The first of these is the programme of requirements of a regional
board for the Certificate of Secondary Education. The South-East
Regional Examination Board has produced a model booklet[1] to
help teachers in schools devise syllabuses which will bear comparison with the Board's Mode 1 syllabuses and thus ensure that
there is conformity of standards of assessment. Within the programme are four key dates, one discretionary and three mandatory. (It simplifies understanding if the term *Year 5* is used to
indicate the academic year in which the examination takes place,
Year 4 the preceding academic year and so on.) These key dates
are:

31 December, Year 3   Statement of intent (discretionary)
1 February, Year 4   Proposed new mode 3 syllabus; specimen
question papers and mark schemes
30 November, Year 5   Draft question papers and mark schemes
First Monday in June, Year 5   Approved question papers, mark
schemes and worked scripts to board; attendance and mark sheets
(for examination) and grade sheets (for course-work) submitted.

These last three dates[2] (I deliberately exclude the statement of
intent because it makes the network unnecessarily long and
complex) represent a chain of events that can be depicted diagram-

[1] *Mode 3: Notes for the Guidance of Teachers* (SEREB, 1973). The importance of parity in standards between modes of examining cannot be over-
estimated. The words 'Mode 1' or 'Mode 3' do not appear on the
certificate, and the board owes it to the user – the employer or the
college of further education – to see 'that grades are neither too easily nor
too hardly earned'.

[2] Known as *Imposed dates* in C.P.A. – 'a date determined by authority
or circumstances outside the network' (British Standards 4335: 1968,
as quoted in Lockyer, op. cit.).

matically as shown below. All these dates represent the final dates for submission to the board. The last date is, of course, not susceptible to much variation, since the written examination must take place in May; but if a school can anticipate the first and second dates, the board will be overjoyed.

Figure 19. Submission events network

The circles are called *events*. Each will later have a number but it would be misleading to give it that number now, since ultimately all events will be numbered sequentially and, as will soon be seen, each of these events, which we can for our purposes designate as 'submission events', will come about only as a result of a series of other events within the school. Letters have therefore been used for reference, though it must be emphasized that lettering plays no part in C.P.A.

The length of the arrow is arbitrary. It bears no relation to the length of time between events. These are shown in weeks, by the figure above the arrow.

Let us now take one of these events, the second, and look in more detail at what goes on within the school to reach this event. Here is a possible sequence of events in 'longhand', as the head of department might put it at a departmental staff meeting:

The draft question papers and mark schemes have to be in to the board by 30 November. As you know there are four of us involved in teaching to this syllabus in year 5. I think we should decide shortly how we tackle the drafting of the question paper. The syllabus is in three parts and it may be that three of us should each tackle one part and pass it round for criticism to the team as a whole. Alternatively one of us could compose the paper as a whole if each member of the team contributes ideas. Will you think about it so that we can decide at our next meeting?

When the paper is drafted we will have to look at it to ensure that it contains an adequate coverage of the syllabus. The mark scheme is the next problem. We must ensure that all reasonable answers are rewarded in the mark scheme. It may be best if someone unconnected with the phrasing of the questions draws up the mark scheme. This may reveal ambiguities in the phrasing of the questions, or imbalance between one question and another. I will volunteer for that task if you like.

We have never before considered pre-testing. It is extremely difficult with a Mode 3 syllabus, since we are unlikely to find another school able to help. However the headmaster made an interesting suggestion at a staff management group meeting the other day. He asked whether we had considered drawing up two questions for each section of a Mode 3 paper as close to each other in style as possible but differing in content, and presenting one in the mock examination and one in the May examination. Unfortunately unless the staff management group agreed to bring the mock examination back to an earlier date in the autumn term, we would not be able to use our findings to ratify or modify our draft paper in time for submission by the set date. Perhaps we should look to see how much earlier the mock would have to be, and whether the idea is worth pursuing.

By the way, we must remember two things. All Mode 3 draft question papers and mark schemes go to the deputy head (curriculum) for vetting. And the office gets snowed under with typing at this time of year. Remember, the school has twelve Mode 3 syllabuses now.

From this – perhaps unrealistically one-sided! – departmental meeting, a sequence of events can be drawn up. The basic network is shown below in Figure 20. This time event numbers have been used. There is a gap in the number sequence for a reason which will become apparent later.

1. Hold departmental planning meeting
2. Draft question paper completed
3. Internal moderation question paper completed
4. Mark scheme prepared
8. Deputy head (curriculum) vetting completed
9. Typing completed
10. Submit to board
B Imposed date for receipt of submission

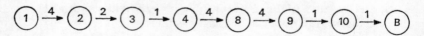

Figure 20. Preparation of question paper events network

Note that the arrow, representing the *activity*, leads to the circle, representing the completed *event*. It therefore takes an estimated four weeks from the departmental planning meeting to the completed draft question paper.

The network duration time can now be established. It is seventeen weeks. Now a consideration arises that is unlikely to obtain in any network of industrial events. There are only twelve weeks between the beginning of the autumn term and the imposed date B. We must do one of two things. We must either revise our event times by these five weeks of *negative float*[1] so that the activity can be contained within the autumn term, or we must place events 1 and 2, at least, in the summer term.

A contraction in the duration time by as much as five weeks is possible, but undesirable. To quote Mervyn Saunders, C.P.A. has 'real value in secondary school organization, particularly in relation to easing the tensions among staff, by bringing some sanity and system to the multiplicity of demands made upon them.' To gain five weeks will undoubtedly impose strain on the department, the deputy head and the clerical staff.

The network falls into two logical sequences of activity: 1 ⟶ 4 , the planning of the question paper; and 4 ⟶ B , the submission of the question paper. Seven weeks' activity can therefore take place in the summer term, leaving ten weeks for the second sequence. We have however, *twelve* weeks in which we can perform the activities of the second sequence. We can now introduce another technique of C.P.A.: the insertion of the *earliest event time* and the *latest event time.*

There are three ways[2] of doing this. The earliest event time may be placed above the circle and the latest event time below; both can be placed below, the earliest within one geometrical symbol, for example, a square and the latest within another, a triangle; or the event circle can be divided into four segments by a cross, with the event number at the base, the earliest event time to the left and the latest event time to the right. Using this last technique, surely the most logical and least confusing, the sequence 4 ⟶ B will now read:

Figure 21. Earliest and latest event times

We are now in a position to look into the possibility of pre-testing with the fifth year. The network is simple:

---

[1] The time by which the duration of an activity must be reduced in order to permit a scheduled date to be achieved (Lockyer, op. cit.).

[2] Lockyer, op. cit., p. 49.

5. Examination taken.
6. Examination marking completed.
7. Results analysed and discussed with deputy head (curriculum).

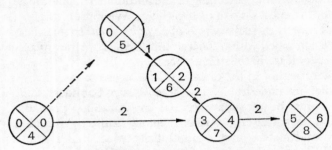

Figure 22. Pre-testing network

Three points emerge from the introduction of this pre-testing network. First we have a *dummy*, represented by a broken line, 'a logical link, a constraint which represents no specific operation'.[1] Secondly we have broken up the *activity* of the deputy head (curriculum) leading to event 8 into two phases, before and after the pre-test. The same time (four weeks) is occupied, but *event 7* is introduced after the first two weeks. Finally, and most important we have had to alter our earliest event time in 8. This is because the sequence 5 ⟶ 7 takes one week longer than the sequence 4 ⟶ 7 . We now have a very simple example of a *critical path*. It is that 'path from a start event to an end event, the total duration of which is not less than that of any other path between the same two events.'[1]

We are now in a position to make certain deductions from our exercise in C.P.A. We are unable to fit into the autumn term all the activities required leading up to the board's imposed date B. It is doubtful whether we would have anticipated this problem except through the use of C.P.A. We would have been faced with another of those 'burning the midnight oil' tasks that would have created anxieties all round.

We know that we *can* hold our pre-testing examination in the autumn term, but that it must be in the first week of term. We can look along the network to see where time may be saved. We are no longer looking, remember, for five weeks. Could the activities leading to events 10 and B not be cut to half a week each? Might not the staff management group discuss with the administrative assistant the phasing of the faculties' typing needs

[1] B.S. 4335 (1968).

for Mode 3 draft question papers? Half to be submitted in the first of the four weeks allocated, and the other half, including this, in the third? Three weeks have been saved. Would the deputy head (curriculum) not be satisfied with one week to look at the draft before the pre-testing? Ah, wait a moment! The network shows at a glance that this makes no difference: our *critical path* does not lie on the horizontal route $4 \longrightarrow 7$.

Three weeks, then, at most might be saved. This would place the mock examinations in the first week of October. The staff management group considers the proposition and turns it down flat. Indeed there is a strong movement towards a much later date for mock examinations. February of the fifth year has been suggested, since decisions on examination entries are no longer being based on results in the mocks, but on half-termly assessments. Despair in the department! Then at a departmental meeting convened to discuss the new situation ('and a fat lot of use your C.P.A. turns out to be!') the voice of the youngest probationer is heard, saying:

'Hey! Look at that network again. Is there anything to stop us pre-testing a representative sample of our questions in one double period in the first week of term? We would be interfering with nobody, and who knows – the kids might even do some revision in the summer holidays.'

Critical path analysis has application to a number of school situations. Often they will involve external agencies: the county education department, for example. A C.P.A. of the network of events and activities leading to the main staffing advertisement for the next academic year will depend on the information on his staffing quota being passed to the headteacher by a certain date. This date, in its turn, depends on a network of events and activities at county level, reaching back both to the approval of estimates by the county council and to information from the Department of Education and Science on the county staffing quota. C.P.A. is, therefore, a management technique which could well be adopted widely by those responsible at county level for staffing. Administrators would then have a clear-cut programme to adhere to. In hit-and-miss administration the 'latest event time' is the date when somebody finally manages to get the job done. However, if that date is one which makes it impossible for the school to perform satisfactorily *its* sequence of events and activities, there will be frustration and stress within the school, and friction and mistrust between the officers of the local education authority and the school.

Bar charts

While C.P.A. has many uses in educational planning, its employment in purely linear situations would be like running a steam-
roller to split peas. A school has many linear situations. Let us
take a report evening for the parents of one school year as an
example.

There are two, independent chains of events. There is the
compilation of the report, which consists of the sequence for each
pupil:

    1a Subject teacher writes report and passes it to tutor.
    1b Tutor collates subject reports, and writes tutor report.
    1c Year head discusses completed reports with tutors.

There is the invitation of the parents, which consists of the
sequence:

    2a Year head drafts and issues letter of invitation asking parents
        to indicate the time of the evening most convenient to them.
    2b Tutor draws up timetable of interviews.
    2c Tutor communicates interview time to parents.

When the two sequences of events are placed end on, as in Figure
23,[1] the duration time of the total operation is five weeks plus.

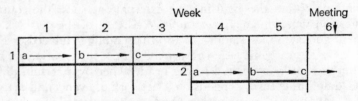

Figure 23. Sequence of events

That is close on half a term, and it can be argued with some justice
that the tutor meets the parents with an out-of-date subject
report. Because the sequences are independent, why should they
not overlap? Provided event 1c is completed before the meeting
there is no reason at all why they should not. We will plan for
sequence 1 and sequence 2 (excluding 2c) to finish together by the
end of week 5. (See Figure 24.)

Before we finally accept this as the best plan, however, let us
look at the people involved in the two sequences of events, to see

---

[1] This is a very simple example of a *bar* or *Gantt chart* used in business
management planning.

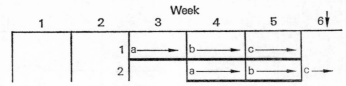

Figure 24. Shortened duration time

how they will fare. When the two sequences were end on, nobody could possibly be involved in events in the sequences at the same time. And now?

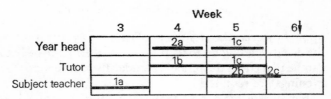

Figure 25. Effect on staff

In Figure 25 it can be seen that the tutor is involved in two operations at the same time. He is engaged in discussing his completed reports with the year head (1c) at the same time as he is drawing up his timetable of interviews (2b). Perhaps this is too heavy a commitment for the same week, particularly as the tutor has a full teaching load, and has to crowd both these activities into his 'free' periods. Indeed, if we look again, we may decide that there is a good reason for separating these two events. Might not discussion with the year head reveal problem cases that determine the position on the timetable of interviews with certain parents so that they fall when the year head is available for consultation?

A shift back of a week for sequence 1 gives the *year head* two tasks in the same week! However, 2a is a task that can be subdivided. The letter can be drafted earlier (2a1). Indeed it should be, since its typing and duplication involve office staff. The second part, the issue of the letter, is a formality (2a2). The final chart is shown in Figure 26.

This bar chart is capable of adaptation to whatever routine a school wishes to adopt. If, for example, all subject teacher reports have to be seen by the appropriate heads of department before they go to tutors, then that event will have to be inserted into the sequence, either lengthening the operation, or reducing the time available for one or more events in the sequence. Once decided

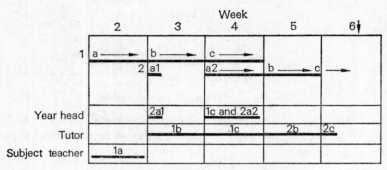

Figure 26. Optimum sequence of events

upon, however, the chart is applicable to every report evening and the events leading up to it. It becomes a template or pattern, which can be placed on the school calendar for the year as often as report evenings are required.

Bar charts have a widespread application to school routines. Every operational sequence that involves staff with different functions benefits from the explicit demonstration of 'who does what and when'. The double chart in Figure 26, with time as the horizontal axis, and event and responsibility below one another as the vertical axis, achieves this objective. This example used two interdependent event sequences, in order to demonstrate how that interdependency can be manipulated. Almost every administrative routine in the school consists of a sequence of events:

the setting of internal examinations;
half-termly assessments;
the completion of entry forms for public examinations;
the production of a school play or concert;
a school journey, educational visit or stay at a field-study centre;
the submission of higher education applications;
decisions on fourth-year options;
the planning of a sports day;
budgeting for the next financial year;
the construction of the timetable.

It is plain that this technique has intrinsic value in that it sets up a methodical plan. It has valuable side-effects too. It is a communication link, since it becomes readily apparent to the staff as a whole what a particular sequence of events entails. It contributes to staff in-service education, since a demonstration of methodical planning may well encourage the individual member of staff to be more methodical in lesson planning, recording information, and so on.

Perhaps its most important subsidiary value is that, because it presents not an arbitrary time scheme with which any member of staff may quibble but a sequence of events about which any member of staff may make a constructive suggestion, there is engendered a greater feeling of involvement in decision-making.

Calendar chart

The obvious next step in planning is that these separate bar charts must be locked together into a master chart which shows every member of staff what is required of him each week of the term. Magnetic boards and coloured tape[1] are invaluable in this exercise. The planner needs to set up on one board all the bar chart sequences[2] which need collating in the term. From this board he works on to a second board which has on the vertical axis all the members of staff, by *role function* not by name: headteacher, deputy head (curriculum), year head, tutor, head of faculty, subject teacher, administrative assistant, caretaker, for example. He begins with those bar charts which have immutable end dates. He locks into these the movable feasts, like Sports Day. He is in fact doing a timetable exercise, not with classes, subjects, rooms and teachers, but with events and activities. There is the inestimable advantage that on the calendar chart a member of staff *can* do two things at the same time. To be more precise he can perform two or more activities in the same week. What the planner is watching for constantly is that he is not imposing loadings on individual members of staff so onerous that they cease to perform efficiently. He has to remember too that one person may appear on the chart in more than one place because he has more than one role. The head of drama, for instance, is also a subject teacher and involved in a report or assessment network. He may well be a tutor too, involved in a parents' meeting network.

When all the juggling has been done – and, because decisions on the placing of sequences of events are often highly subjective, one would hope for frequent consultation – the calendar chart can be produced. Each school will have its own favoured method of presentation. A permanent layout board in the staffroom, with

---

[1] SASCO Visual Planning supply these.

[2] There is of course no need for him personally to have designed the sequences. The head of drama, for example, is the right person to devise the network leading to a play production: casting, rehearsals, set design and construction, the making of costumes and properties, publicity, front of house arrangements, and so on.

the activities typed on to self-adhesive labels and placed in the
appropriate square of the lattice, is worth considering. A cursor
that slides along the board to indicate the current week anticipates the 'Goodness me! I thought it was only the *fifth* week of
term!' excuse for inaction. Each task can be indicated simply by
the bar number and the activity letter, as in Figure 26, provided
a code is placed prominently alongside the board. After all each
member of staff cannot fail to see that there *is* a task for him in a
particular week. What the task is he can easily check.

The syllabus matrix

Educationists are, on the whole, much given to words and disin-
clined to use graphic representation. Nowhere is this more true
than in syllabus construction. Aims, objectives and method become
inextricably confused in a welter of words, often used with emotive
and subjective undertones and without real precision. We aim to
'encourage a good standard of . . .' but rarely see in the syllabus
how we are to encourage and *what* a good standard is.

Even in, indeed particularly in, the creative-expressive subjects
we must have an analytical approach. There is a confusion
between the subject, which may or may not be 'scientific' (whatever that may mean), and the content, which must be able to
stand up to rigorous scientific investigation regardless of the
subject. For example, if in English we wish to teach letter writing
we need to analyse the topic:

A.   *Purpose*
     application for employment;
     business letter;
     invitation;
     social intercourse;
     commercial: purchase by mail order, complaint, etc.;
     special occasion: congratulations, condolence, etc.

B.   *Approach*
     (*i*) Conventional: (*ii*) Imaginative:
          content   content
          style   style
          vocabulary   vocabulary
          mechanics   mechanics

We now have certain criteria against which to log the assignments to our pupils:

1. Work in pairs. One of you will write to the complaints department of a reputable department store, explaining how a recent purchase has not come up to expectation. The other will write an account to a relative or friend of what was wrong with the purchase, amusing or indignant as you please.
2. Write to the bank manager for an overdraft. Write his reply refusing it.
3. Study one of Lord Chesterfield's letters to his son; Johnson's letter on patronage; one of D. H. Lawrence's or Katherine Mansfield's letters to a friend.
4. You will be shot at dawn. You may write just one letter. You have exactly thirty-three minutes before the firing squad is ready for you.
5. 'Mr and Mrs Golightly have pleasure in inviting you to the wedding of their daughter Gloria to . . .' Reply. Write a week later to Gloria when you hear the wedding is off because he already has a wife and six children.

In half an hour I could devise twice as many more assignments. That is beside the point, however. I should stop and think. How many assignments do I need to meet the criteria I have established? Have I a proper balance in the pedagogic methods I have chosen? Do I need/can I afford the time to cover all the purposes I have listed?

The skilful teacher evaluates his assignments not on the basis of how witty or imaginative they are, but on what they will achieve. One could easily construct a matrix in which A and B were the axes, and tasks 1 to 5 were logged against these axes. Some tasks would appear in more than one section of the matrix. We could then see where there were gaps, where there was replication. We might decide that the gaps were unimportant and the replication desirable or inevitable. Equally our work might bring to light serious shortcomings in our syllabus planning.

The best use of syllabus matrices that I have encountered recently is in the Schools Council 14–18 Geography Project,[1] an example of which is shown in Figure 27. Increasingly, major curricular schemes are being devised using this technique. It is

[1] I am indebted to Derek Gray, Kent Co-ordinator of phase II of the project, and a number of enthusiastic Kent geography teachers for permission to reproduce this example; and to Dr Gladys Hickman, John Reynolds and Harry Tolley, successively directors of the project, for their development of curricular concepts which led to this form of syllabus presentation.

	Settlement	*Agriculture and land use*
Local area	Urban zones (1) Site factors (& physical) Changing growth factors – town and country Shopping patterns and surveys Journey to school Spheres of influence	The farm as a system (1) Farm study (& field work) Changes in land use (postwar)
Local area and British Isles	Urban zones (2) Christaller – hierarchy & threshold Decay & renewal New towns Conurbations Settlement in East Anglia and Anglesey	Von Thunen theory and application Marginal land Alice Coleman's model Changing land use National Parks
Other developed regions	Dutch polders/ Canadian Prairies	Irrigation – Languedoc Government action, e.g. virgin land in Kazakhstan T.V.A. Extensive farming Prairies Sydney area land use
Less developed regions	Third World cities e.g. Ibadan and Calcutta	The farm as a system (2) Subsistence (e.g. small- holding in Sri Lanka, & Nigeria and Kenya) Plantation agriculture – (changes in Malaya since 1960) Von Thunen – Pampas Multi-purpose Scheme – e.g. Damodar
World context	Millionaire cities Primate cities Rank/size rule Classification by function Distribution	Soil erosion/conservation Pioneer fringes Co-operative systems– China and U.S.S.R. (collective)

Figure 27. Syllabus matrix – Geography taught

Industry	Transport	Population
Classification of type Location factors Distribution	Journey to school Urban transport Accessibility New road systems Commuter problems Airport game	
Location factors Heavy industry (iron & steel game) Light industry (location game) Development Areas, e.g. North East; South Wales Growth industries – petro-chemicals Weber	Suitability of type Time/distance/cost relationships Motorway networks New links, e.g. Severn Bridge, & Humber Bridge simulation Vertiport for Smaithe city – simulation South-East networks	Areas of decrease: Wales & N.W. Scotland Areas of increase: S.E. England Immigration (intra & inter) Migration and mobility
Primary industry (e.g. in Australia) Dupreville simulation Industry in north-east U.S.A.	Interface – Channel crossings San Francisco problems European canals – Rhine (E.E.C.) N. American – St Lawrence Airport location	Europe – axis of growth Migrant workers Sequent occupance, diffusion N. America; Australia
HEP — development in e.g. W. Africa (Volta) Egypt (Aswan) Tourism (E. Africa) Multi-purpose adjustment	Development of net- works and patterns Brazilian Railway Development Ghana railways Alaska	Problems of growth Age/sex pyramids Diet and malnutrition Depopulation in S. Italy Pressure & response (Hong Kong) Pressure – China, El Salvador, Japan
Pollution The energy crunch	Suitability of type Scale Energy crunch Air and ocean routes Panama and Suez canals Problems of Concorde	Pyramids World distribution Government decisions World contrasts in income, diet, poverty, density, growth rate, etc.

on a conceptual basis, to fourth and fifth years

so simple that it can be applied even to sections of an ordinary school syllabus, with the great advantage that the rigour of the technique imposes objectivity in evaluation.[1]

Conclusion

In themselves, techniques are valueless: at best toys for those with leisure, a category in which few teachers fall today. In the hands of the skilled practitioner, these techniques become tools. Yet even now their value is problematical. Tools can be handled skilfully but with ignoble purpose. It is finally to the mind of the educationist that we must turn. The aims conceived there must always determine the course of action we take, the use we make of our tools. External constraints – the availability of resources, the effect of the social or political climate in which we operate, for example – may force us to modify our immediate objectives. Our aims, given that our educational philosophy is sound, remain.

[1] An example of a complete Child Care syllabus, using this technique, is given in Appendix 2.

9 Pressures for change

Every school is a dynamic social organization and, as such, in a constant state of change. The purpose of educational management is to equip a school with the skills and techniques that enable it to assimilate that change, and turn it to advantage.

Change is more likely to originate from external than internal pressures. The existence of such pressures and the degree to which they can be modified lie largely outside the sphere of influence of the school. Nevertheless, because the ability to respond constructively is crucial to the successful operation of the school, no book on educational management could conclude without a survey of a representative sample of these pressures, and the response to them.

Political pressure

This book is not concerned with party politics. It is concerned, however, with national educational policy which, whatever the swing of the pendulum of political power, has pursued a reasonably consistent course towards comprehensive reorganization. The failure of this Secretary of State to give approval to one county's plan for reorganization, the pressure of that Secretary of State on another county to submit its plan for reorganization, the arguments for the retention, abolition or adaptation of the direct grant schools, are all peripheral to the main trend. By 1972 a total of 1591 of all secondary schools in England and Wales were comprehensive, and contained over 36 per cent of the pupil population of the relevant age group. By the academic year 1974–75, according to the *Times Educational Supplement* survey of comprehensive reorganization in the 104 English and Welsh education authorities that resulted from the April 1974 revision of local government, 'the proportion of children in comprehensive schools is now 70 per cent'. Sixty-five of these authorities have between 70 and 100 per cent of their secondary children in comprehensives.[1] It comes as something of a shock to realize that the comprehensive 'experiment', as some writers still term it, has been going on for a quarter of a century.

There is one major difference, however, in what has happened in the past ten years. Before the issue of circular 10/65 most schools were willing partners in the change. Many comprehensive schools were purpose-built, established in areas of new residential development or as replacements for schools long overdue for closure. A considerable number made the adaptation gradually, by the introduction of unselected intakes in the lowest age group. Such schools were able to respond methodically to the demands placed on them by the need to restructure the curriculum, the pastoral organization, or the staffing of the school. Their main problem indeed was that they grew imperceptibly – if there was not foresight – from an organization of a size and type that could be run, or appear to be run, by one style of educational management into one where all too often frictions developed, communications broke down and disaffection set in.

The increased pace of reorganization led to 'shot-gun marriages'. Changes in political control led to stop–go situations. Both, while doing little to affect the overall situation, exacerbated the feelings of frustration and bitterness in the teaching profession, and the bewilderment of the general public. Local education authorities were themselves much harassed. One chief education officer, it was popularly supposed, kept in his desk a multiplicity of folders labelled:

Reorganization scheme – Labour Council under Labour Government

Reorganization scheme – Conservative Council under Labour Government

Reorganization scheme – Labour Council under Conservative Government

and so on. The story certainly illustrates the dissipation of the resources of time and energy which ought properly to have been brought to bear on purely educational issues.

Uncertainty of the future is probably the greatest disincentive to successful adaptation to new situations. There has been far too much uncertainty for parents, pupils but, above all, for staff. The headteacher-designate of any new comprehensive school should

[1] From Mark Vaughan's analysis in the *Times Educational Supplement*, (21 March 1975).

be appointed a full year in advance. Education officers, no doubt circumscribed in their actions by rigorous financial stringency, and often by committees lacking in any perception of the demands of educational management, have rarely been able to do this. If the appointee is the head of one of the existing schools, he should be relieved of his current responsibility. Wherever possible his temporary successor should be someone who will have a post in the new school, and who knows the nature of that post, so that he can work within the present structure towards the planned change. Too often one of two situations prevails in schools due for closure. Either they become moribund, seemingly determined to die of inertia, or they decide to 'go down with all flags flying', nobly perhaps but misguidedly.

Existing staff must know their place in the new structure. This means that the determination of the new structure must be an overriding priority. Yet no incoming headteacher can possibly decide his structure without a sound appraisal of the local situation, though he is all too frequently expected to do so. Though he may be quite clear as to his aims, the ordering of his objectives is subject to modification. Every headteacher in this situation is faced with a dilemma: whether to introduce the minimum of change and run the risk of having the new school cast willy-nilly in the mould of its predecessors; or whether to be radical and run the risk of having his objectives misconstrued through lack of understanding or resistance to change, or both.

Should the headteacher be appointed from one of the schools to be reorganized, he is no less in need of this time for appraisal. Perhaps he is in greater need, since he has been so deeply immersed in the previous situation that he requires even more the opportunity to think, to look around him and to discuss.

The basic prerequisites for successful reorganization are these:

1. The aims and objectives of the new school must be established and communicated.
2. Those who will be part of the new school, staff, pupils and parents, must know what is happening, what is expected of them, and to what extent they will from the outset be able to participate in its development.
3. The organizational machinery for the smooth running of the establishment must be conceived and set in motion.

No headteacher can achieve these aims in isolation. He needs the support of the local education authority. (How many have an officer or adviser with special responsibility for helping the headteacher to make contact with the correct agency in the seemingly hydra-headed county education office?) As the pieces of the jigsaw that will make up the new school fall into place he needs the helpful criticism of those already within the community and the no less helpful stimulus of those who come from without. Far too many comprehensive schools are still struggling, perhaps five or more years after they opened, to recover ground lost through early mismanagement.

The best example of forward planning for secondary reorganization that I have encountered recently was in Marple, Cheshire. From the existing grammar and modern schools two comprehensive schools, Marple Hall and Marple Ridge were to be created. The headteachers-designate were appointed at least a year in advance. They worked closely together, backed by a local education authority[1] wise enough to give support where it was wanted without needless interference.

The heads of both schools issued working papers to their prospective staff as planning documents, designed to involve them progressively in the decision-making process. Derek Saville, headmaster of Marple Hall, presented his working paper as a challenge to his staff to identify the aims of the new comprehensive school:

> In setting up a new school . . . formed from the amalgamation of our two single-sex grammar schools . . . we need to consider the general nature and educational purpose of a comprehensive school, together with the specific aims of such a school established in this particular location.
>
> As grammar schools, the two institutions were charged with precise aims . . . to prepare and train the brightest children . . . to take their places in suitable social and professional milieux. But in future we shall have a more diffuse set of aims. While the nature of our intake will broaden, geographically it shrinks and becomes altogether more local. Necessarily, we shall become a microcosm of the community which engenders us.

In contrast David Styan, headmaster of Marple Ridge, sets out his aims for the staff to discuss and debate :

> To create a caring environment in which everyone recognizes the value of warm personal relationships.

[1] A situation even more praiseworthy in view of the fact that local government reorganization was taking place at the same time. In April 1974 the local education authority became the new Metropolitan District of Stockport.

To value every individual and to encourage an awareness of the needs of others, and a response to them.

To foster an appetite for learning, both individually and in collaboration with others, for creating, participating, sharing new experiences and developing self-discipline, initiative, responsibility and perseverance.

To involve children, staff, parents and the community in the life-long process of education, and to help equip everyone for life in a dynamic society.

To ensure that everyone achieves some degree of success, to value all kinds of achievement, and to learn to cope with failure, and that to err is human.

To identify the needs of both children and staff so that they may derive satisfaction from their work and progress in their chosen careers.

These aims can be summarized as care, involvement and achievement.

I have made clear in the opening chapter that there can be no educational progress if a school has no clearly defined aims, well presented, and capable of being understood. However any of us might re-phrase David Styan's aims to suit our own temperaments, conditions and philosophies, nobody would question that they fulfil these criteria.

From the basis of their first working papers these two head-masters were able to proceed steadily to the more detailed planning of their curricular and pastoral structure, the schools' roles as community schools, their relationship with feeder schools and each other, and the precise allocation of roles within their schools. As early as November 1973, Marple Ridge High School was able to send out to parents a newsletter *Progress Report No. 1*, as vital a step as any in this process of change. Over the following months, staff, pupils and parents were increasingly involved in the restructuring of the secondary educational provision in Marple. In February a full day conference for the staff of both schools, which I was invited to address, seemed singularly lacking in the stress that normally precedes such drastic reorganization. There was concern for the future, naturally, particularly that academic standards could and would be maintained; but the general atmosphere was one of confidence and participation.

It is not in any way to detract from the efforts of the head-masters and their staff to point out that here was a local education authority keenly aware of its role in reorganization: to be supportive without being interfering. Many of those reading this section who have been involved in reorganization will regard what I have described as an 'out of this world' situation. It ought to be the norm.

The contribution of teacher training

No college or department of education would, I believe, like to see itself regarded as a source of pressure for change. Nevertheless, if it is properly performing its role of disseminating new curricular concepts and involving its students in forward-looking educational experiences, it must be such a source.

No college could rest content with educating its students merely for the present in education. For one thing, one school's present is another school's distant past – and yet another school's unforeseeable future! While recognizing that its students will have to go out into the *status quo*, whatever that may prove to be, the college must inculcate some educational idealism. Students must be familiarized with the areas of change.

I am indebted to a German educationist[1] who has studied the English educational scene in considerable depth for this summary of the responsibilities of the training establishment to the students who are to become the next generation of secondary teachers:

He should be helped to abandon preconceived ideas about 'types of children', 'ability ranges' . . . and so on; instead he should learn to see the importance of the individual child and his particular needs in the academic as well as the social sphere.

He should be prepared to teach the whole ability range, preferably and increasingly in mixed-ability groups. This means knowing about the interrelations of children of differing abilities in learning situations, using new teaching methods (group and individual work), mastering adequate teaching and learning aids, or even preparing his own materials.

He should be made aware of his pastoral role and enabled to take an active part in the social organisation of the school, including guidance and counselling.

He should be encouraged to work in teams and develop an overall sense of cooperation not only with his colleagues . . . but also with pupils and parents.

He should be enabled to participate in the innovation process . . . especially in the field of curriculum reform.

He should be made competent to take his part in the democratic process of decision-making within the school.

[1] Dr Annegret Körner, a lecturer in education at the University of Geissen. At the time of writing, she is involved in a research project on comprehensive education and teacher training.

It seems self-evident that every student who has been exposed to these educational ideas, not one of which does not echo ideas propounded in one chapter or another of this book, will act as a pressure for change upon the school – a pressure for which the college is responsible or may take the credit, whichever you prefer. Even a school which believes that it subscribes to the principles enunciated here will have staff who will be resistant to the suggestion that newly qualified teachers 'hardly dry behind the ears' will be equipped to make the contribution that Dr Körner implies. Conversely there will be new teachers whose enthusiasms for innovation outrun common sense and moderation.

Perhaps the most valuable feature of our national system for teacher training is that a substantial part of it takes place in schools, in the context of realism, often grim realism, not idealism. For the receptive school there is much value in an on-going relationship with a college or department which enables school and training establishment to cross-fertilize theory and experience. For many schools the pressure which I describe in this section can be both refreshing and beneficial.

Curricular development

The most significant external influences on the curriculum of the grammar school were traditionally the examination boards and the universities. The former largely determined what was to be taught although the best grammar schools, it must in all fairness be stated, taught well beyond the requirements of the boards. The universities determined both the standards to be attained and, in many instances, the subjects to be included in the syllabus. The arts/science division in the sixth form, which Guy Neave[1] suggests has been considerably eroded by the greater flexibility offered in comprehensive school sixth-form curricula, arose originally from the strictures imposed by university expectations.

The advent of the C.S.E. in 1965 thrust upon schools a responsibility for involvement in deciding the content of the curriculum which many teachers had been demanding for some time. A number threw themselves with gusto into the construction of a host of Mode 1 syllabuses. The teacher-controlled subject panel of one board produced a history syllabus susceptible, by a combination of different periods of study with different topics, to over a hundred variations. The problems of standardization of results

[1] Guy Neave, *How They Fared: the Impact of the Comprehensive School on the University* (Routledge & Kegan Paul, 1975).

within a board, let alone among boards, were largely overlooked
in the enthusiasms of liberation.

Year	Subject entries (to nearest thousand)	% of all entries
1966	49 000	8·9
1967	70 000	9·6
1968	94 000	10·7
1969	122 000	11·8
1970	143 000	12·7
1971	165 000	13·3
1972	209 000	14·8
1973	245 000	16·3
1974	477 000	21·0
1975	543 000	22·4

Figure 28. C.S.E. Mode 3 subject entries

Initially there was much surprise and some regret that the school-
based Mode 3 option was not taken up more widely. There
should not have been, since many schools at this stage found the
syllabuses created by their colleagues broadly satisfying. It was
only as the Mode 1 syllabuses began to ossify, or to be subjected
to limitations based not on educational considerations but administrative expediency, that Mode 3 syllabuses became far more
widely introduced, as the statistics in Figure 28 show. The basic
principle of the C.S.E., after all, is to examine what is being
taught, not to cause to be taught what it is desired to examine.
But the devising of a Mode 3 syllabus is not a simple task. It
requires of teachers skills in the management of curricular material
that only a handful had previously acquired. Bloom's *Taxonomy
of Educational Objectives*[1] became the book title most widely
used by all who aspired to devise Mode 3 syllabuses. It is
doubtful if all who refer to it have read it.

[1] Bloom, B. S., *et al.*, *Taxonomy of Educational Objectives: the Classification
of Educational Goals*, Handbooks I and II (Longmans Green, 1956 and
1964).

Whatever the shortcomings of its syllabuses, Mode 1 or Mode 3, the C.S.E. examination hurled our schools into a field of activity of unimagined complexity. It is no exaggeration to say that it profoundly affected the management of schools, in the timing of the examination, the utilization of staff in the examination process, and above all in the thrust it gave to the momentum of curricular innovation. For all this schools were singularly unprepared.

The C.S.E. examination was not the only curriculum development to impose pressure upon the school. Through the Schools Council, the Nuffield Foundation and a galaxy of other sponsors came new curricular projects. Most of these were based at universities, a few at colleges of education. Obviously the project directors sought out those schools where their projects were most likely to thrive, the very schools, needless to say, already in the forefront of curriculum innovation. Most curriculum projects have a two- or three-year pilot phase before they can be disseminated more widely. A number of schools which embarked on projects found that, at the very time when the project could be of most use to the school, that is when the wrinkles had been ironed out, the member of staff most involved in the project moved on, often to a promotion resulting from his involvement in the project.

Curriculum projects brought considerable pressures to bear on the school organization. There was a tendency for local education authorities to look to an innovatory school when a further innovation was proposed. For both schools and l.e.a.s a certain prestige attaches to being considered co-operative in curriculum development. For the school there was often money available for new equipment or materials, sometimes even a staffing bonus. Few considered seriously enough whether the benefits would outweigh the stresses.

It is obvious that somebody must experiment if there is to be educational progress. The problem is one of cost-effectiveness. Unfortunately there is no way in educational management of assessing this by the yardsticks of profit or productivity, as in business. A school can only avoid the undesirable pressures and attract the desired pressures of curricular innovation if it has a clearly defined overall curriculum development plan. No such plan will have the precision of a town development plan, with plots neatly earmarked for extension in this or that month of such a year. But it will readily disclose the fertile areas.

Education authorities should require of its schools development plans, not merely so that they can measure achievement against

expectation – an essential feature in management by objectives –
but so that they can see those areas in each school which will best
respond to the stimulus of an external curriculum project. Curriculum growth must be organic, but that does not mean that it
cannot benefit from unforeseen opportunity. Nevertheless the
overriding principle is that the school's curriculum must respond
to the needs of the pupils. However attractive the project, it
should only be entered upon when it is advantageous, desirable
and above all manageable.

At the time of writing we seem to be nearing the end of the
expansive phase of curriculum projects based on new concepts,
content and methodology. The pressures of the current lustrum
or decade will be to create less divisive systems of assessment at
16+ and 18+. The syllabuses for a single system of examination
at 16+, for the Certificate of Extended Education and for whatever finally supersedes A level do not need extensive research.
They lie before us in profusion. What is now required is selection
from that material suited to different ages and abilities, and
experimentation in methods of assessment. Here too there will be
pressures upon the school. Already many are involved in pre-
testing, in operating joint C.S.E./G.C.E. board syllabuses, or in
providing facilities for objective tests whereby the standards of
any new examination will be moderated. These pressures are
unlikely to impose so great a strain upon a school's resources.
Equally they are unlikely to produce the stimulation of the best
of the curricular innovations.

Community involvement

Just as in critical path analysis there is *negative float*, so perhaps
there can be negative involvement. That is the first impression
one forms of the pressure, or lack of it, imposed on our educational
system by the community in this country. We make comparisons
with the U.S.A. and, though we may heave a sigh of relief that
we are not subject to the vagaries of community control on the
school's finances, staffing establishment or admission of pupils, we
nevertheless lose something in community concern for education.
Most European countries have moved far more rapidly that we
have to what many would consider the true comprehensive school,
that which the community considers its own.

I have for a quarter of a century been involved in, and an
advocate for community schools. I have come in that time to
believe that the community school concept must be very much

more even than education from the cradle to the grave, as Henry Morris[1] visualized it. We have widened our interpretation of the content and range of education remarkably in the past twenty-five years. We have only sporadically succeeded in reaching out to the community we serve so that that community is involved in educational change.

The principle reason for this lack of involvement is that there has been little encouragement from the school or the educational system to this end. Traditionally our schools have been set apart from society. Ritualized allegiance, through Old Boys' Societies and the like, has been encouraged, but this amounts to very little in terms of genuine participation. When the school is 'threatened' with reorganization or dissolution, then the rallying cry can be heard 'Hands off *our* school'. Strange to say, there have been few occasions when that cry was heard – at least loudly enough for anyone to hear outside the immediate locality – for a school other than a grammar school.

One can identify in these campaigns against reorganization a genuine attachment to those grammar schools, both as they were when the parent generation attended them and as they are at the time when they are threatened with closure. Nevertheless the managerial skills with which these campaigns are mounted should not be allowed to deceive us into thinking that they represent an expression of community feeling. They represent the feelings of only a small but vociferous section of the community. And so it is with their opponents, it must be said. 'Stop the Eleven Plus' is no more a genuine popular movement than 'Save our Grammar Schools'.

The community as a whole has been, in most parts of the country, signally unconcerned with its secondary schools. As one lives in a community and becomes integrated with it, one becomes aware that there is a deep-rooted alienation from schools in general. The price we pay today for our divisive educational system of the past is that a majority of the members of the parent generation regard themselves as school non-achievers, regardless of what they may have achieved since they left school. Whatever the new school claims to be offering to all its students, they believe, because it is their experience, that all schools must be devices for rejection. For the perpetuation of this belief educationists bear much responsibility. It is they who stress constantly achievement at school rather than achievement in living.

[1] See Harry Rée, *Henry Morris: Educator Extraordinary* (Longmans, 1973), and my own *The School and the Community* (Macmillan, 1971).

It does seem, then, that the onus lies on the school to demonstrate that it is open to the community. In Chapters 6 and 7 I have
written of the importance of communication, but if there is to be
genuine education for change it is not enough that we merely
communicate. We must be involved in the community if the
community is to be involved in the school. In many ways the dice
are loaded against this involvement. In inner urban conditions
teachers are often unable to live anywhere near the school, sometimes because they cannot afford to, but usually because there is
little encouragement from the local authority for them to do so.
Except in the New Towns, the very idea that teachers might be
considered key workers and given housing priority has been, until
recently, treated with derision. Only now, as urban authorities
find themselves in an educational crisis, in part of their own
making, is there any indication of a change of policy.

Even where social conditions are conducive to the teacher
living in the community the tradition of the last half-century, at
the very least, militates against his involvement. The archetypal
village schoolmaster who was 'an integral part of the close-knit
community he served' no longer exists.[1] Succeeding generations of
teachers felt it incumbent on themselves to maintain social distance
from the parents of the children they taught.

The increased mobility of the teaching profession has been
much blamed in recent years for a lack of identification between
teacher and community. It is, of course, a factor. There is no
such thing as *a* community, as John Eggleston[2] has pointed out,
but a series of more or less overlapping 'associations'; for work, for
living, for leisure. It is through contact in one or more of these
associations that a sense of community is engendered. It is possible,
however, that Eggleston's observation, important though it is,
overlooks two developments in present-day society affecting the
school's relationship with its community. The first is that we now
have in our schools as young teachers a generation which, regardless of present political beliefs, cannot fail to have been influenced
by the militancy of large numbers of students in the events of the
late 1960s in Paris, Amsterdam, London and California. Student

[1] In the first few paragraphs of 'The head and the community school'
in *Headship in the 1970's* (Blackwell, 1968), from which this quotation
comes, I recreated briefly from the school log books and school board
minute books something of the life and times of Samuel Hollins, for most
of his adult life headmaster of a nineteenth-century Cambridgeshire
village school.

[2] S. J. Eggleston, *The Social Context of the School* (Routledge & Kegan
Paul, 1967).

internationalism, by no means confined to the followers of the writings of Marcuse, Lukacs and Sartre, has made it far easier for our young teachers to relate without inhibitions to their own generation in the community. Though this may make them a little suspect to some in the parent generation, for most they are a welcome change from that breed of teacher which attempts still to stand on a pedestal that no longer exists.

Secondly it is possible for there to be a relationship between an institution and a community, even though it can only be expressed in inter-personal relationships. Consequently if the school proclaims an ideology which is relevant to the aspirations of the community then it relates to the community even though the teachers within the school move on. It goes without saying that their successors must not only subscribe to the ideology, but be seen to subscribe to it. There is evidence of this continuity in the community's growing recognition of the *caring school*, as distinct from the school with a number of caring teachers in it.

Community involvement will be expressed in action and not in words, and by an increasing number of individuals and extant groups rather than by organized pressure groups. It is precisely this which worries so many headteachers and their senior staff. They do not see how they will 'manage' this outside intervention in what they regard as their affairs. Their concept of management is wrong if they cannot get beyond the idea of *inside* and *outside*, and the conviction that *manage* means *manipulate*. If there is to be, as a consequence of the school's outreach into the community, a corresponding 'inreach' of the community into the school, then a healthy management system will respond to it. Those of us who have experienced this involvement find that it consists in the main of a desire to help the school in practical ways rather than to be a part of any decision-making machinery. None the less when ideas are forthcoming which may have bearing on the direction in which the school may go or the speed at which it may move, it is well to heed them. After all, schools do not have a monopoly of wisdom.

Conclusion

Whatever the impact of external pressures for change may be, the more regarded pressure should always be that which comes from within the institution. If the institution is dynamic, then management, to be effective, must be dynamic. Those concerned with management – and it has been a theme of this book that management is a function of the school staff as a whole, not merely of those appointed to managerial roles – must constantly be re-examining the strengths and weaknesses of the organization. As objectives are achieved, new objectives must be established. As weaknesses are discovered, steps must be taken to eradicate them.

By ourselves we are nothing. However able we may be as individuals, we are engaged in a corporate enterprise, and our most valuable resource is mutual support. There is no place for suspicion, the shelving of responsibility, the avoidance of uncomfortable situations. Good management depends not merely on sound policies, but on the proper motivation of those who will carry out the policies. There is no sounder motivation than a belief that the organization is humane, concerned and confident.

10 Education for management

Since schools are so obviously concerned with management and in this respect are no different from any other social organization, is it not somewhat surprising that so little attention has been paid, until recently, to education for management? It was not until 1967 that the first real attempt was made. The Department of Education and Science established a small team, mainly of Her Majesty's Inspectors, under the title of the Committee on the Organisation, Staffing and Management of Schools (COSMOS). The task assigned to the team was 'to mount a quick series of short courses, to consider longer term solutions of the problem and to collect or create material and devise methods through which new skills might be developed'.[1] The main objective of these courses was a limited one, 'an examination in depth of the use of resources, particularly those of teaching power and time'. From this there evolved the technique known as curriculum analysis, whereby schools are able easily to investigate their use of resources and to decide the cost, in terms of manpower, of innovations. It does not matter whether these innovations derive from a desire to restructure the curriculum, are a result of organizational change, or stem from proposals to allow staff more time for planning or pastoral care. The technique has been codified by T. I. Davies;[2] but further research has simplified it considerably, so that the basic principles can be learnt in a day.

Murray White rightly points out that 'in the early years, the courses were almost certainly vulnerable to the charge of elevating a potentially useful technique into an end in itself'. The efficient use of resources is only one element in the management of secondary schools. There is considerable danger of the more humane objectives becoming subordinated to this mechanistic objective. There has, however, been a growing number of courses

[1] W. Murray White, HMI, 'Courses for management', *Secondary Education* (June 1974).
[2] T. I. Davies, *School Organisation* (Pergamon, 1969).

designed to examine interpersonal relationships, to study problems typical of those found in secondary schools. The lecture/discussion group/plenary session syndrome has given way to open-ended discussion, skilfully led by tutors, in which the experience of course members can be fully utilized.

Courses in educational management have been organized since the end of the 1960s on a national basis mainly by the Department of Education and Science, the Advisory Centre for Education (ACE), the College of Preceptors and Loughborough Summer School and on a regional basis by university schools or institutes of education, polytechnics and, increasingly, local education authorities themselves. These courses, however good they may be, suffer from four major weaknesses: there is no co-ordination between them, and consequently the range of what is understood by the organizers to be implied by 'educational management' is great; they do not provide sufficient places for all those who wish to attend them, let alone all those who need them; most operate on a multiplicity of levels, when there is strong evidence that they would be more effective if aimed specifically at top management (heads and deputies), middle curricular management (heads of faculty and of department) and middle pastoral management (heads of years and of houses); and, finally, operating in isolation, they are not backed up by the necessary research and experimentation.

Ron Glatter in his excellent book[1] argues cogently for the establishment of development centres in educational management. He sees the centre's functions as five-fold:

> (a) to conduct research into administrative processes and problems in education . . .
> (b) to undertake development work to examine the applicability of management systems and 'techniques' . . .
> (c) to . . . develop effective training methods . . .
> (d) to disseminate the results of (a) and (b) and the materials developed in (c)
> (e) to offer directly a limited number of courses, workshops and other training activities . . .

Advocates of a staff college for training for headship and other senior posts in schools will find here strong support for their case, though they may be less than satisfied when they learn that Glatter

[1] Ron Glatter, *Management Development for the Education Profession* (Harrap, 1972). Most of Chapter 5 'A plan for development' is devoted to a detailed study of the purpose, number and staffing of development centres.

believes that all these tasks have equal value and should command an equal share of resources. I myself believe that this is, on the whole, a correct policy, though the immediate pressure to meet the demands for (e) might lead initially to some difference in weighting. The most valuable part of the proposal lies in the inter-locking of research and educational practice.

So far only one such development centre has been established, at Padgate College of Education, Warrington, under the auspices of a consortium of local education authorities. Many education-ists await with interest an account of its work so far, and some evaluation of the extent to which it has achieved its prime objec-tives. Meanwhile its director, Fred Tye, must from time to time cast a longing and envious eye at Ron Glatter's proposal that such a centre 'would need at least twelve professional staff'.

Probably the most interesting of the long-term courses so far devised by a polytechnic is the Diploma in Management Studies (Education Management) of the North East London Polytechnic. The course has been devised by the Department of Management in the Public Services, based at the Anglian Regional Manage-ment Centre, Danbury, in collaboration with a major local educa-tion authority, Essex. The course is designed for those occupying positions of management responsibility in educational organization in the tertiary sector, in schools and in local authorities. The needs of the course member, as seen by those who have constructed the course, are worth quoting extensively:[1]

> (i) he requires the educative process to provide him with the opportunity to change and develop attitudes, and acquire skills and knowledge to enable him to assess the validity of his and his organization's objectives and performance;
> (ii) he requires that . . . he will be a more effective manager at the conclusion of the course;
> (iii) he requires a meaningful dialogue with managers from re-lated sectors on matters of common concern, but not at the expense of demonstrable application of ideas to his own problem areas;
> (iv) he requires the process to take place in a manner which is likely to cause him and his organization the least dislocation, in terms of release, and render the maximum advantage;
> (v) he requires accreditation . . .

The course is modular and can be taken in one year of full-time study, or up to four years of part-time. Its objectives, syllabus and methodology have a relevance and an immediacy which are sadly

[1] *Proposals for the Diploma in Management Studies (Education Management)*, N.E. London Polytechnic.

lacking in the courses for teachers currently being organized by the schools of management in many universities and polytechnics.

Nevertheless, in view of our past neglect, however much these full-time courses may multiply, it is to vacation and in-service courses that we must direct the bulk of our necessarily limited resources. These will, of course, be more superficial, but they may provide the initial impetus for teachers to read further, to investigate different management systems or curricular developments in neighbouring schools, and in general to systematize their thinking about education.

The philosophy of educational management

The true problems of living – in politics, economics, education, marriage, etc. – are always problems of overcoming or reconciling opposites. They are divergent problems and have no solution in the ordinary sense of the word. They demand of man not merely the employment of his reasoning powers but the commitment of his whole personality. Naturally, spurious solutions, by way of a clever formula, are always being put forward; but they never work for long because they invariably neglect one of the two opposites and thus lose the very quality of human life. In economics, the solution offered may provide for freedom but not for planning, or vice versa. In industrial organisation, it may provide for discipline but not for workers' participation in management, or vice versa. In politics, it might provide for leadership without democracy or, again, for democracy without leadership.[1]

The relevance of these words to educational management cannot be overstated. Schools are concerned with freedom and planning, with discipline and participation, with leadership and democracy, not merely in what they teach, but in the way they function as organizations. They too live a lie if they pontificate in one manner, but perform in another.

The importance of educational management, then, goes far beyond the effective functioning of the institution. It must act as a vehicle for the commitment of man's whole personality, as Schumacher puts it. Harry Rée[2] once summarized the role of the head as someone who 'is called upon successively, and indeed sometimes simultaneously, to play [these parts]: listener, encourager, dissuader, reporter, watcher, judge, critic, decision-taker and on occasions commander.'

[1] E. F. Schumacher, *Small is Beautiful* (Sphere Books, 1974).
[2] In *Headship in the 1970s*, ed. Bryan Allen (Blackwell, 1968).

Real as these functions are, they are only aspects of one man's personality and they lack the holistic concept, implicit in Schumacher's thesis. Furthermore Rée's definition, by over-stressing the charismatic qualities of leadership, undervalues the merits of collective responsibility.

Educational management may use techniques, but it is not the New Technology. Unless it is under-pinned by sound conceptual thinking it will lead teachers to mistake the structure for the reality. Whatever the form of educational management, whatever the institutions in which education for management may be conducted, if we fail to clarify our aims and intentions we will achieve little or nothing.

Appendix 1

Some organizational structures

SCHOOL A

School A was until 1970 a secondary-modern school with fewer than 200 pupils. Its development as a comprehensive school began with a five-form-entry first-year (11+) intake. The size of its staff as a secondary-modern school made the title of head of department little more than a fiction for the payment of a post of responsibility allowance: most were one-man or one-woman departments. As the school increased in size and as its curriculum broadened, departments became more functional. At the same time the headteacher's concern to develop a system for pastoral care led to the establishment of a house structure. Of necessity some heads of department were also heads of house. This had the merit of emphasizing the interrelationship of pastoral care and academic progress, but blurred role definitions.

In normal circumstances the problems of dual responsibility would have ironed themselves out as the school grew to its planned size of 850 to 900. Unfortunately local administrative and demographic considerations reduced the annual entry, already small for an effective 11 to 18 comprehensive school, to at first four and later barely over three forms of entry. Although the head had points available he did not have the staffing vacancies to enable him to regularize his structure even on a pastoral/departmental basis. In 1975 the structure looked like this:

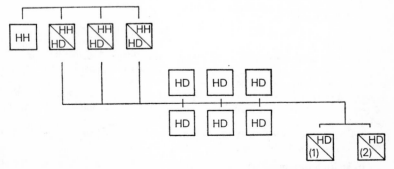

(1) Head of (embryonic) sixth.year
(2) Curriculum co—ordinator

This is a situation, regrettably by no means rare, in which organizational planning is wholly at the mercy of circumstances.

SCHOOL B

School B is a grammar school for boys expected to:

(a) amalgamate with a grammar school for girls;
(b) absorb a co-educational secondary-modern school;
(c) receive an eight-form-entry first-year (11+) comprehensive intake.

Which event will take place first is not yet known. They may even coincide.

The headmaster, appointed some years ago in anticipation of reorganization (and still waiting), inherited what was then a traditional grammar-school structure which had heads of department for 'major' subjects and masters in charge of 'minor' subjects. In the interim he has introduced two structural changes: the abolition of this distinction, and the institution of a pastoral system. As yet most pastoral staff still have curricular responsibility.

He plans to change on reorganization to a faculty structure. The reasons he gives show a combination of educational philosophy, managerial skill and the recognition of sheer practicalities:

(a) A departmental structure fragments knowledge, undesirable in a selective school, unthinkable in a comprehensive school. Put positively, a faculty structure facilitates subject integration.

(b) A faculty structure, as a 'new broom', will make easier the amalgamation of the staff of three schools.

(c) Points will be available for the separation of curricular and pastoral responsibilities.

(d) Sixteen heads of department (probably more after reorganization) cannot meet effectively as a curriculum development team.

(e) The building extensions and adaptations provide the physical conditions for a faculty organization.

His planned structure has five faculties (Mathematics, Science, Communication, Humanities and Creative Subjects) with physical education and remedial education outside the faculty structure.

SCHOOL C

School C is an established eight-form-entry comprehensive (11 to 18) school. It has a seven-faculty structure, with fairly typical subject groupings. Curriculum co-ordination is the responsibility of a director of studies, and it is through him that heads of faculties have their main line of communication to the senior management of the school: the headteacher, the deputies and the senior teachers.

In the diagram only two faculties have been fully detailed. The Communications faculty has three features of interest:

(a) It includes business studies which, if it contains commerce, is at least as much a humanities subject; or, if bookkeeping, a mathematics subject.

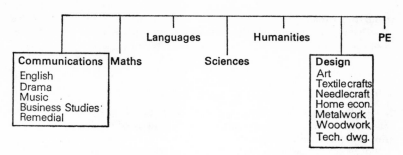

(*b*) Languages form an independent faculty, although French is as much a communications subject as English. This may be because its inclusion would overweight the faculty, or because languages are particularly strong in the school.

(*c*) The placing of remedial suggests that its role is confined to the development of literacy, and that the Mathematics faculty has its own staff for the problems of numeracy.

The Design faculty has a considerable and praiseworthy breadth. The inclusion of home economics highlights one of the problems of faculty groupings. It has the least affinity with other subjects in the group (though by no means none, if well taught). Nevertheless it may have been 'attracted in' by its traditional affinity with needlecraft, which is most properly a Design subject.

SCHOOL D

School D is an upper (13 to 18) comprehensive school, with an eight- to ten-form entry. It has one of the most adventurously experimental curricular structures I have encountered. It has a typical departmental organization, but sixteen departments are linked within a *three*-faculty system.

(*a*) Science, Technology, Design
(*b*) Humanities, English
(*c*) Mathematics, Languages, Leisure Pursuits.

No intrinsic logic is claimed for the faculty groupings: they are convenient 'containers' for approximately equal numbers of staff and for equal curriculum units. Each faculty has command of three half-days of the curriculum. There are two consequences of this. The first is that four and a half days of the week are timetabled within the three 'container' units, leaving one half-day to provide the necessary elasticity for some courses or some pupils. The second is that, in this 13 + school, the three years of compulsory schooling absorb four and a half days of a subject teacher's time. Obviously, should the teacher have departmental or pastoral responsibility, or an allocation of sixth-year teaching, he will *not* be involved, or not wholly involved, in the allocation of all three years; but these are easily arranged variations of a norm. Each faculty is run by a co-ordinator (as in School E) and is self-operating for staff cover and timetabling. Plainly no co-ordinator is going to be regarded as an expert in all the subjects in his faculty. As a result he may be all the more effective as a facilitator of interdisciplinary studies and a balanced system of options.

SCHOOL E

School E is, like school D, an upper (thirteen to eighteen) comprehensive school, of the same size and maturity. It is structured deliberately to combine a departmental with a faculty system.

There are six faculties and eleven departments. Department heads are responsible to a 'co-ordinator'. The latter is also clearly responsible, as the diagram demonstrates, for his 'own' subject (there is, for example, no head of department for French or history) and for some subjects which do not warrant departmental status (for there are more than eleven 'satellite' subjects).

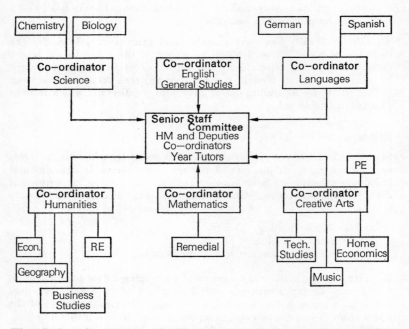

The placing of remedial under the mathematics co-ordinator is puzzling, unless, unlike School C, remedial literacy is the province of English specialists.

Appendix 2

Child Care syllabus

Aims

This is a two-year course for students in the fourth and fifth years of secondary education and aims at:

(a) Preparation for marriage and parenthood emphasizing the importance of a happy, stable home and a planned family.

(b) Providing some understanding of the normal stages of child development and children's play.

(c) Encouraging awareness of the needs of the community, mainly through work in pre-school playgroups.

(d) Developing wide practical skills needed in the domestic care of children.

Objectives

The student is required to:

(a) Recognize stages of development: social, physical, intellectual, emotional, spiritual.
    Appreciate play/social/emotional needs at each stage.
    Suggest ways of meeting needs at home, and in playgroup.
    Show in practice that this learning has been assimilated.

(b) Read and study an approved topic on own initiative.
    Write about topic, explaining factors clearly, and selecting relevant illustrations.

(c) Understand why and demonstrate how to:

    (i)   make a toy
    (ii) make a child's garment
    (iii) make a picture book
    (iv) prepare and serve a family meal.

(d) Keep a record of own observations of a child over a period of time.
    Present clearly with appropriate illustrations.
    Make practical use of observations in relationship with child.

Content

The course will include:

(a) Theory and practical work with babies and pre-school children at home and in playgroup.

(b) Practical sessions which include:

     (i)   attendance and observation at pre-school playgroups
     (ii) making play equipment
     (iii) preparation and serving of toddler's meals
     (iv) making and care of children's clothes.
(c) Visits to hospitals, children's homes, children's library and pre-school playgroups.
(d) Films and talks by experts (e.g. health visitor) whenever possible.
(e) (i)   special studies
     (ii) child study
     (iii) project on a special topic such as rising fives; parent participation in playgroups; play study; playgroup survey.
(f) Course-work including termly tests, diary of playgroup visits, writing of original stories, reviewing children's books.

	Value of play	Development → 2 yrs	Development 2–5 yrs	Health and nutrition	Baby care and clothing	Reproduction	Language Development	First aid and safety	Children with problems	Personal relationships
Exposition	Lecture Guided reading	Lectures Films Guided reading Health visitor	Lectures Films Reading (children growing up)	Demonstration Reading	Lectures	Lectures (Health visitor)	Lectures Reading Library visit	Demonstration of artificial respiration Lectures RoSPA films	Guided reading	
Observation	School Child Care Unit	Visits from mothers with babies	School Child Care Unit Photographs	Magazines Advertising	Advertising Shopping	Film	With Child Care Unit and in playgroups Book display		Video-tape	
Discussion	Questions, interview, reporting on visits	Free discussion	With teacher and with nursery nurses		Informal exhibition	In small groups	In class	Questions on Child Care Unit	'Thumbnail sketches' to read and discuss	In small groups
Written work	Playgroup diary Worksheets	Coursework diagrams	Coursework Worksheets	Worksheets	Worksheets	Worksheets	Child's story	Reporting	Coursework	
Practical	Playgroup visits (approx. ½ term) Making a toy	Out of school	Assignments in Child Care Unit and playgroups	Cookery: family meal, party tea, picnic	Making a child's garment		Interview Story-telling	Playgroups		In playgroups In family

Book-list

The number of books written in this country on educational management in *schools* is depressingly few. Many American books throw some light on the topic, but for the general reader the search for what is, for him, the wheat will take him through a great deal of chaff; and for practising teachers time is always at a premium.

A. A. Coulson has compiled recently – unfortunately almost too recently for my purposes – an excellent 'select annotated bibliography', *School Administration and Management* (Flag Publications, Hull, 1975). Almost all the books I mention below are inevitably included in his bibliography; but I have limited this list to what I regard as key books.

Writers on Organisations, edited by D. S. Pugh, D. J. Hickson and C. R. Hinings (Penguin, 1971), is an exemplary introduction to the general theories of management. The editors summarize without prejudice.

Two books with the same title, *The Sociology of Education*, one by O. Banks (Batsford, 1971), the other by P. W. Musgrave (Methuen, 1972), while healthily contrasting in viewpoint and style, provide a sound starting-point from which the reader may formulate his personal concepts of management theory.

Secondary School Administration: a Management Approach, edited by M. G. Hughes (Pergamon, 1970), is valuable, but suffers because too many contributors begin with management theory and seek to apply it to the school situation. In contrast I have taken the view that the management needs of the school must first be established; only then should management theory be investigated in depth to discover what is either directly relevant or seminal.

Headship in the 1970s, edited by J. B. L. Allen (Blackwell, 1968), remains one of the most readable books on the practice of educational management, though none of its contributors attempts to propound any significantly original educational theory. The merit of the book lies in the fact that the majority of its contributors write from direct experience.

Running a School by C. H. Barry and F. Tye (Temple Smith, 1972) was the first book – as distinct from symposium – to deal with the organizational management of secondary schools from within. It is wise, it is written with great clarity and simplicity and a wealth of illustrative case-studies, but it has two major weaknesses: it adopts management by objectives too uncritically; and there is little evidence that anyone other than the head may be concerned with running a school except in so far as the head wills it.

The books in the present series, Heinemann Organization in Schools Series, are all relevant and interrelated. Details appear on the dust jacket. Several, notably Keith Blackburn's *The Tutor* and Michael Marland's *Head of Department* and *Pastoral Care* themselves contain useful book-lists.

Index